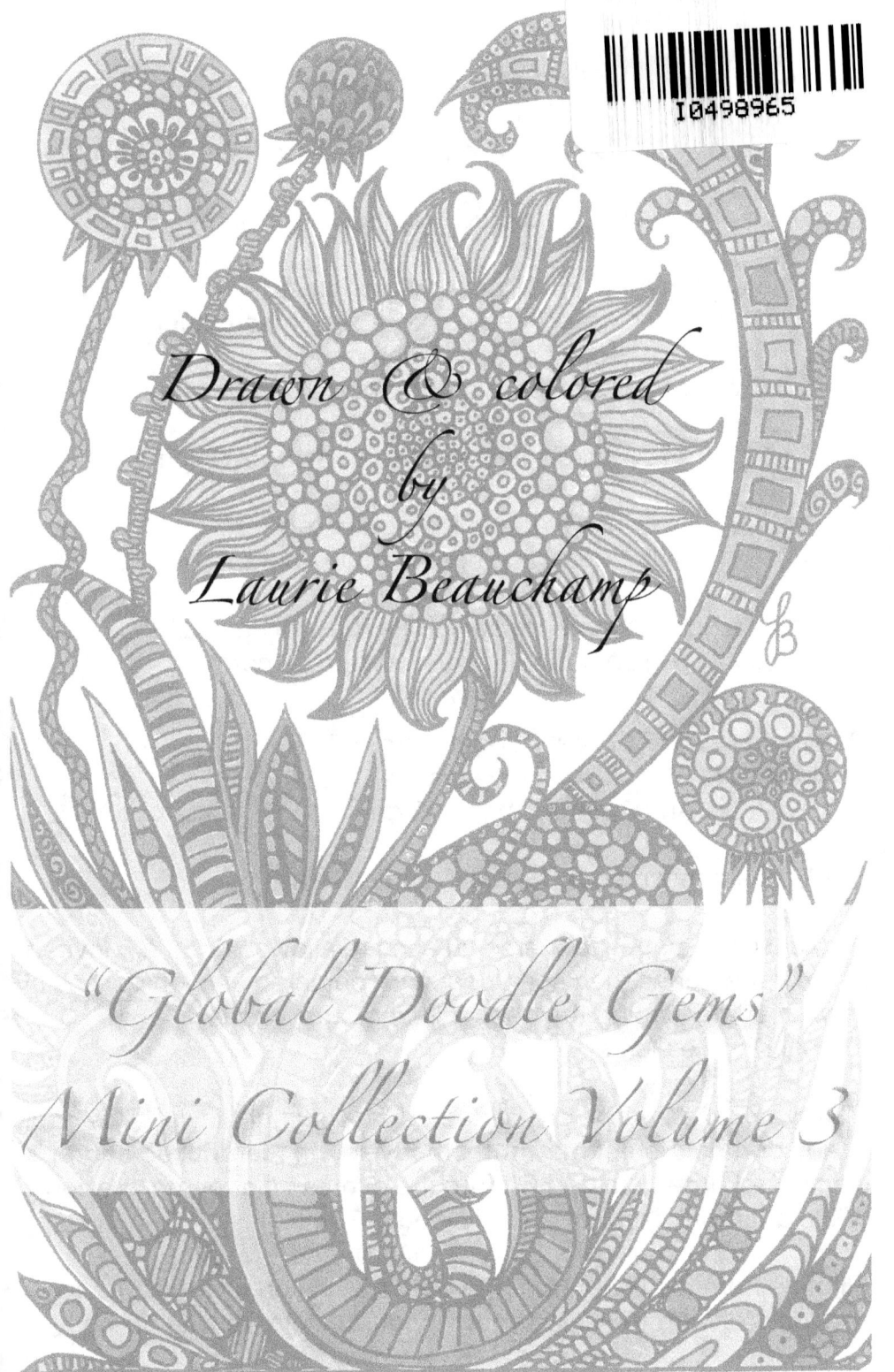

Share your colored versions with us !

The Official FB book page, stay on top of what we have in the works !
www.facebook.com/globaldoodlegems

The Community group, share your colored pages, meet the artists, enjoy exclusive freebies, take part in community Charity books and so much more......
www.facebook.com/groups/globaldoodlegems/

Follow us on Twitter.... @GlobalDoodlegem

We are on Instagram too
@globaldoodlegems for instagram

...and if you are not social like that we have a blog
globaldoodlegems.wordpress.com

Copyright © 2015 Global Doodle Gems
Published by Global Doodle Gems
Anna-Marie Vibeke Wedel

All rights are reserved by Global Doodle Gems.

Duplication of pages for personal use are allowed. You are invited to color the pages then scan/post your coloured versions to social networks, mentioning the book title and author/artist
(Global Doodle Gems).

All artwork and images are protected by copyright laws. This book or any portion thereof may not, otherwise, be reproduced and/or distributed or transmitted without the express written permission of the artist/publisher of Global Doodle Gems.

All of us from the Global Doodle Gems wish you a colortastic time and look forward to seeing your wonderful color results online !

Published by
"GDG"©
Global Doodle Gems

Contributing Artists
"Global Doodle Gems"
Mini Collection Volume 3
Thank you for your contributions

Pica Wu, Nadège Zenfeerie, Asma Zergui,
T.J., Rover Hsiao,
Lynne McGee, Laurie Beauchamp,
Johanna Ans, Jenny Wei,
Jane Levi, Jane & Yaya,
Iben Lykke Højholdt,
Yaya, Creative Rosalien,
DomDomx, Dianne Comeau, Diana Holmes,
Audrey Sagh, Nicole Whelan
and
Ondine Summers

Contributing Artist
Pica Wu
Taiwan

Facebook : picapicadrow2

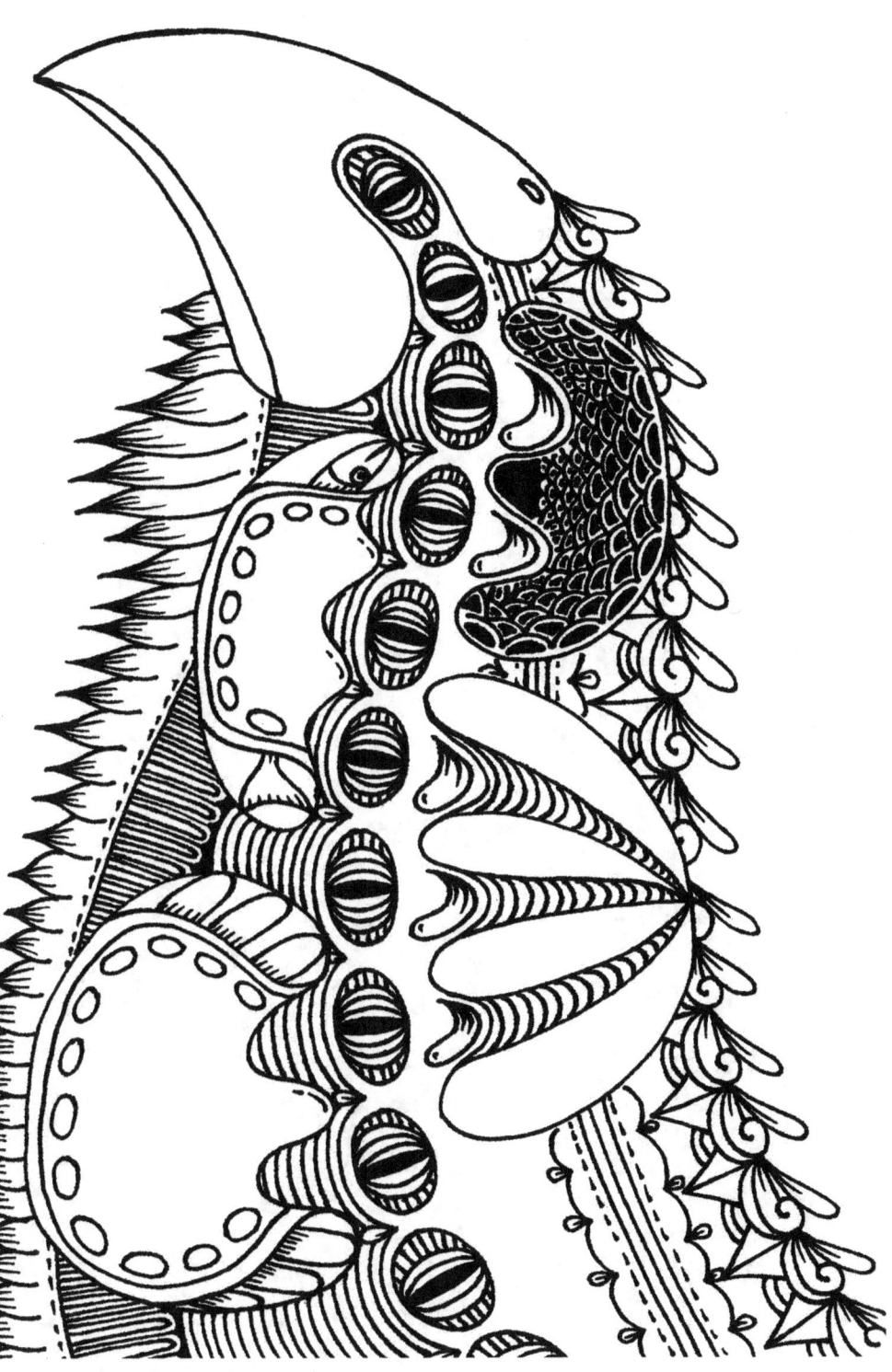

Contributing Artist
Nadège Zenfeerie
France

Facebook : zenfeerie

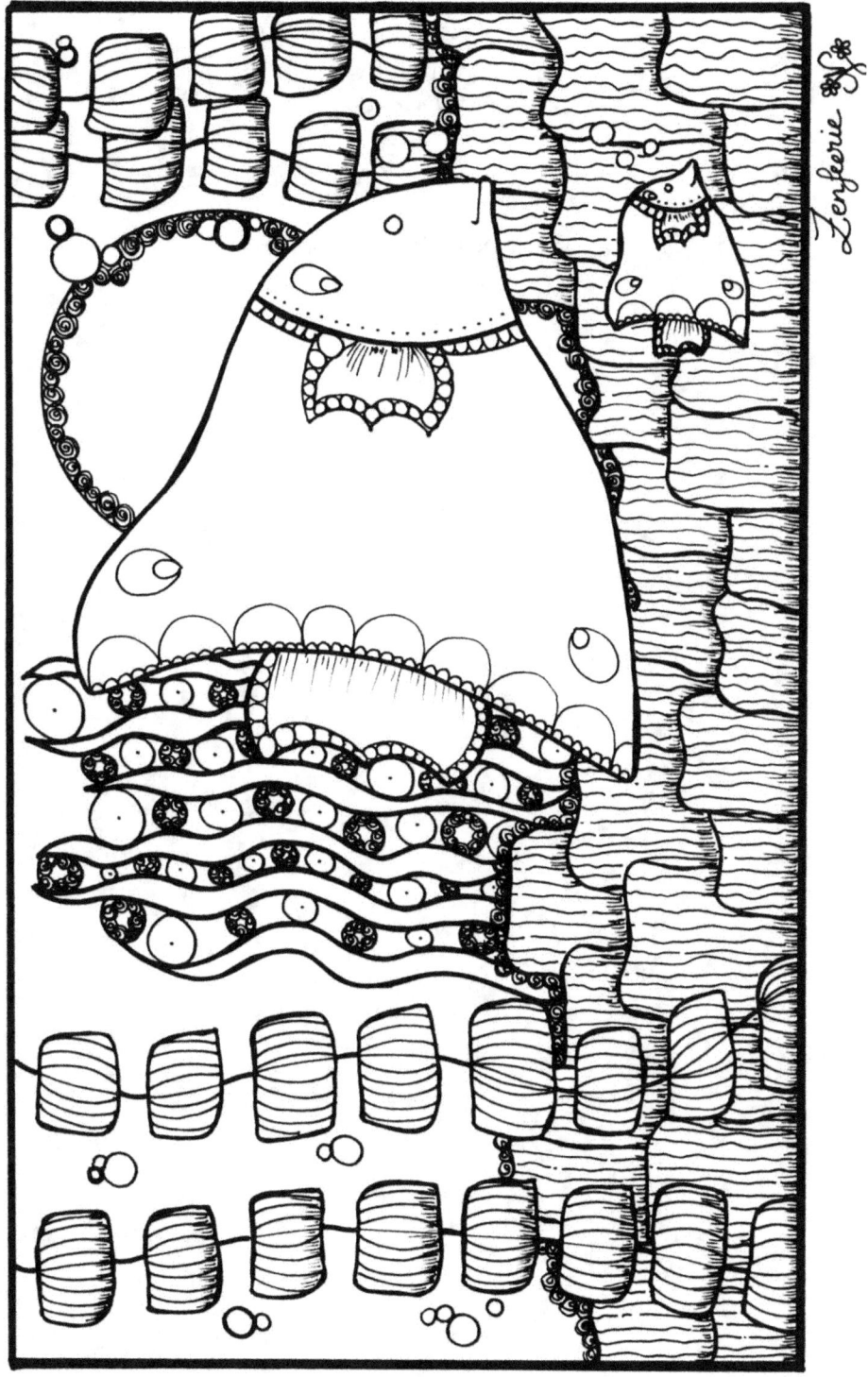

Contributing Artist
Nadège Zenfeerie
France

Facebook : zenfeerie

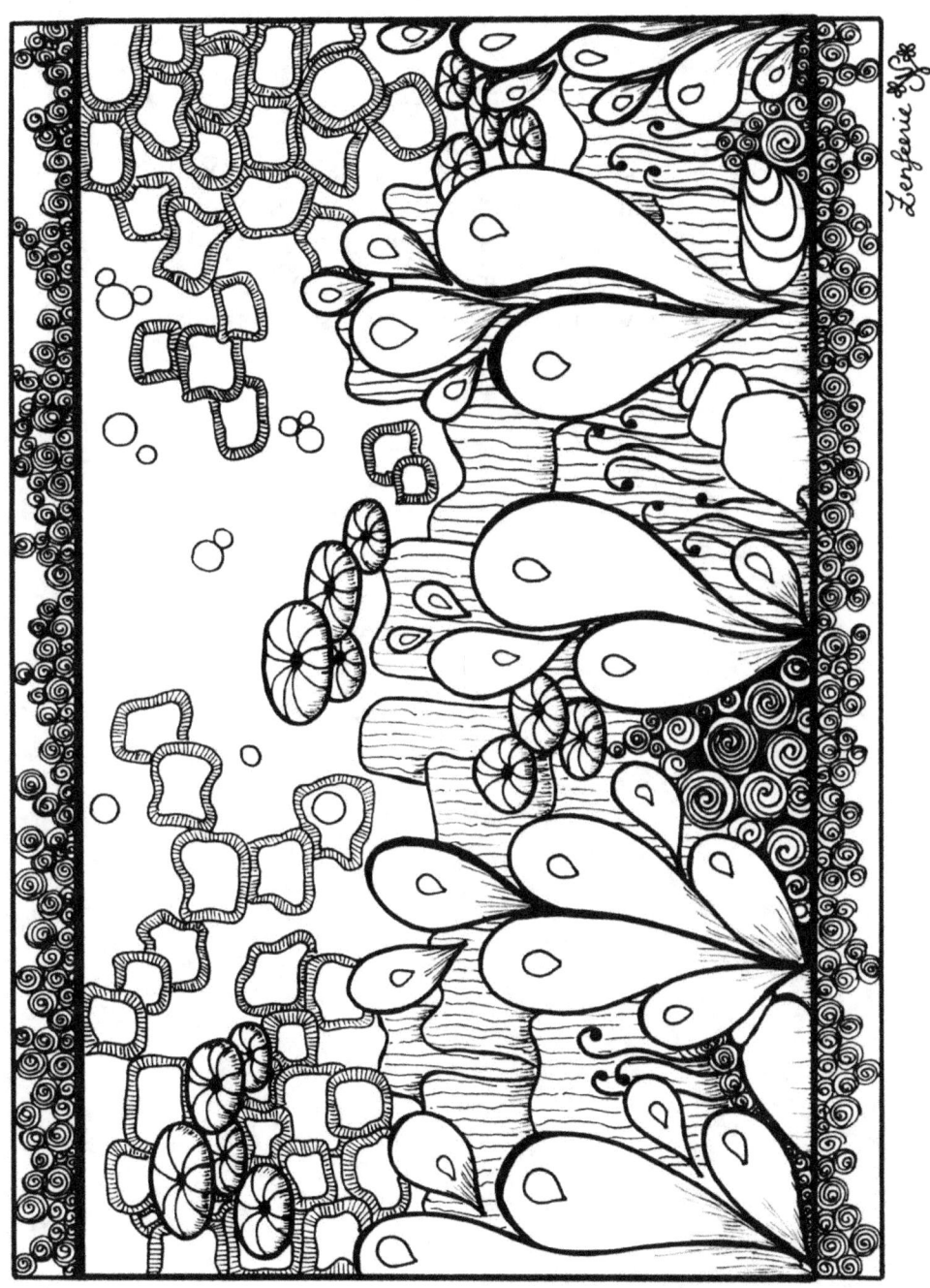

Contributing Artist
Asma Zergui
Algeria

Facebook Group : coloringbooksandmandalas
http://www.asmazergui.com/
Etsy shop : coloringbooksadults
Society6 shop : asmazergui
http://www.amazon.com/Mrs-Asma-Zergui

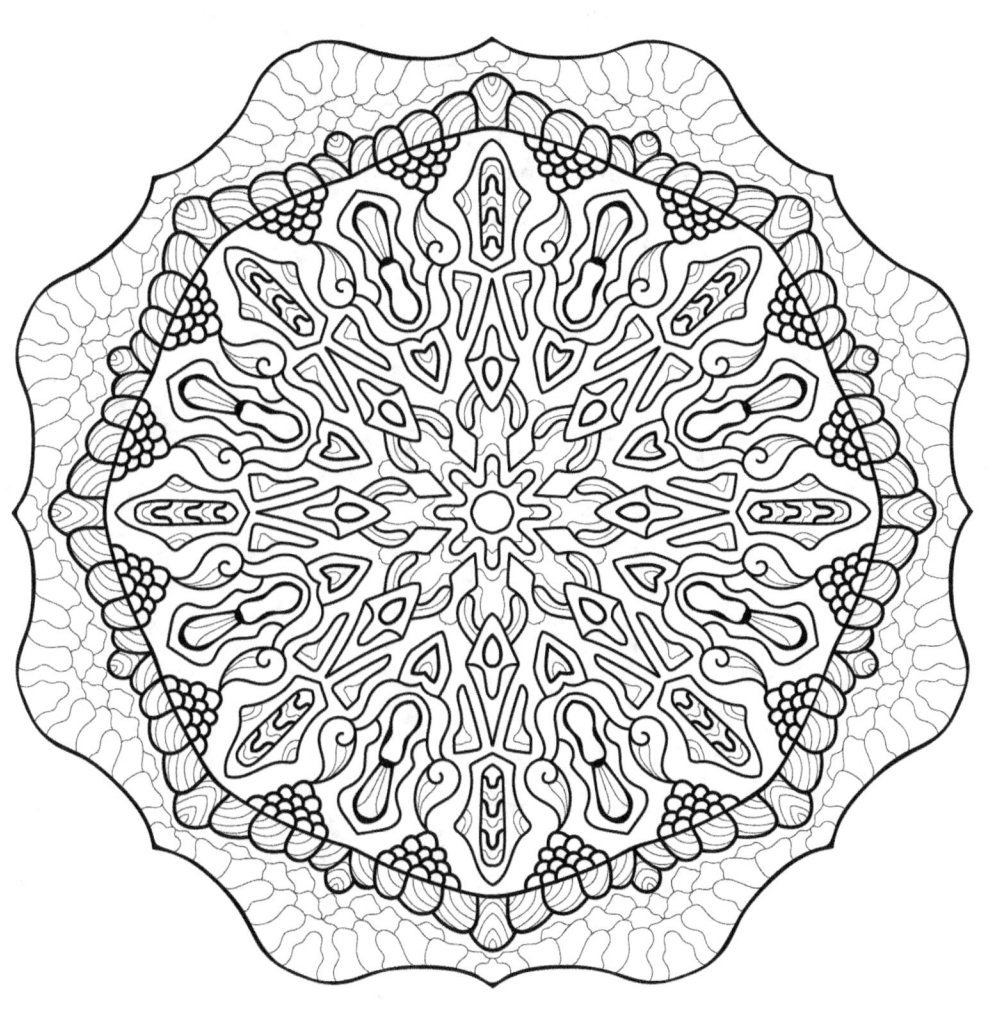

Contributing Artist
Asma Zergui
Algeria

Facebook Group : coloringbooksandmandalas
http://www.asmazergui.com/
Etsy shop : coloringbooksadults
Society6 shop : asmazergui
http://www.amazon.com/Mrs-Asma-Zergui

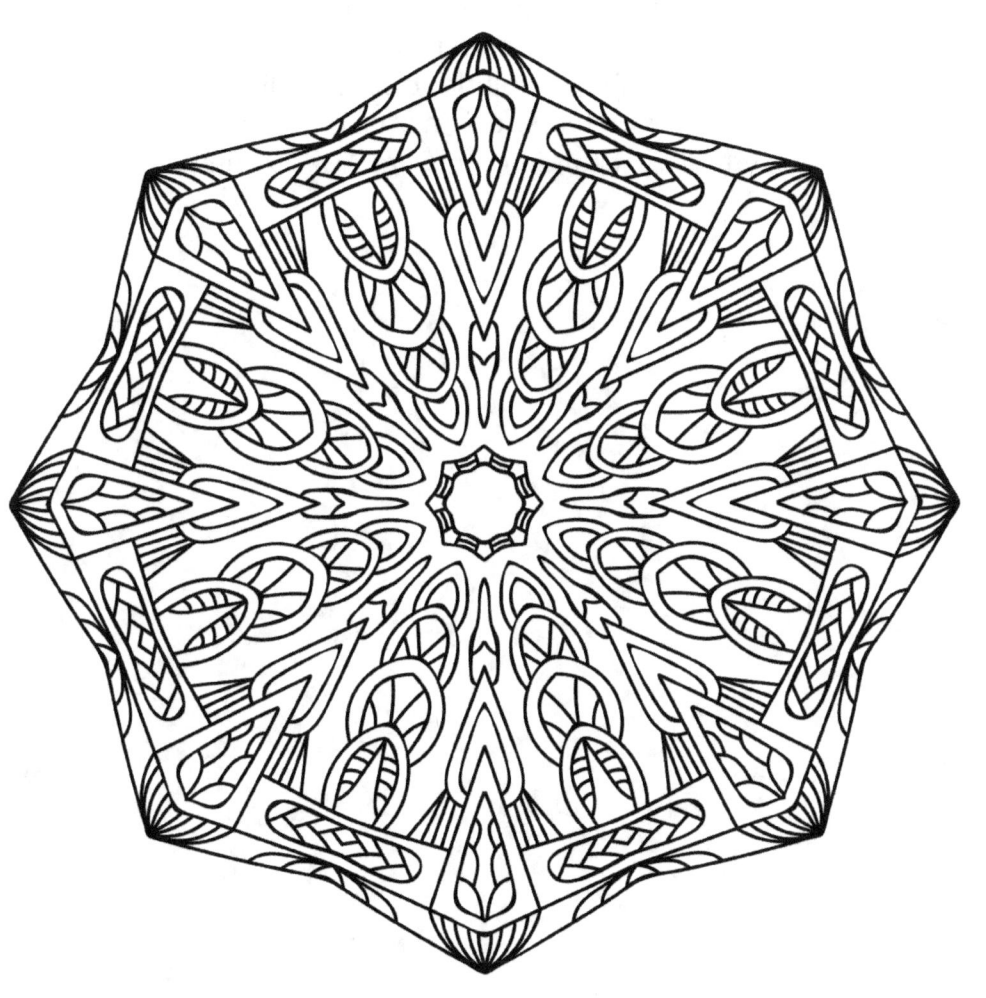

Contributing Artist
Asma Zergui
Algeria

Facebook Group : coloringbooksandmandalas
http://www.asmazergui.com/
Etsy shop : coloringbooksadults
Society6 shop : asmazergui
http://www.amazon.com/Mrs-Asma-Zergui

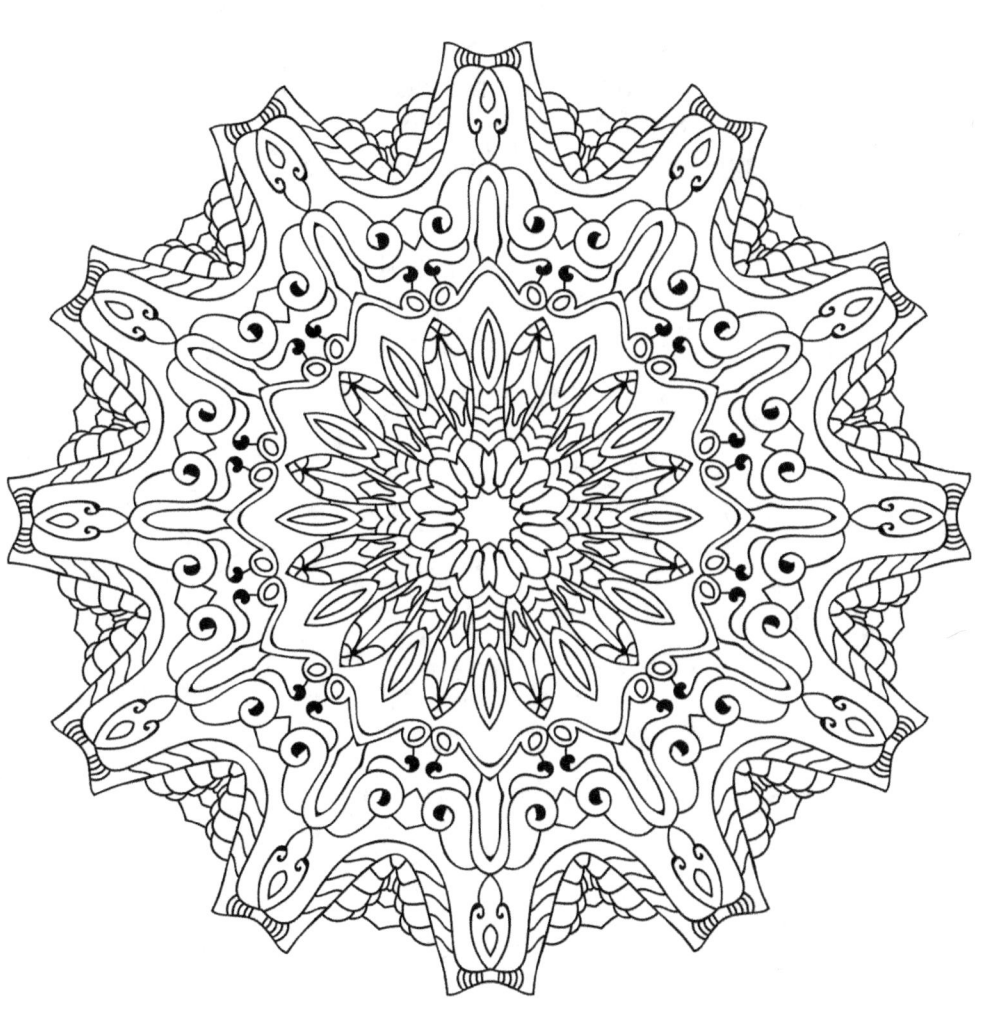

Contributing Artist
Asma Zergui
Algeria

Facebook Group : coloringbooksandmandalas
http://www.asmazergui.com/
Etsy shop : coloringbooksadults
Society6 shop : asmazergui
http://www.amazon.com/Mrs-Asma-Zergui

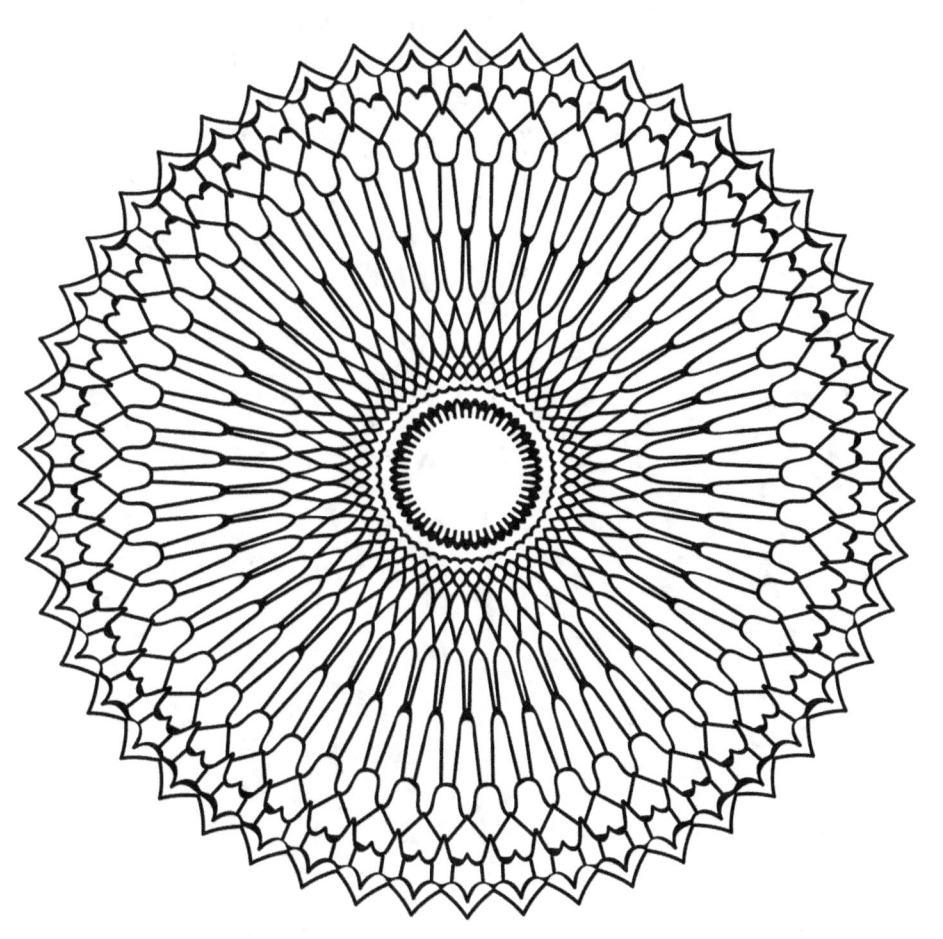

Contributing Artist
Asma Zergui
Algeria

Facebook Group : coloringbooksandmandalas
http://www.asmazergui.com/
Etsy shop : coloringbooksadults
Society6 shop : asmazergui
http://www.amazon.com/Mrs-Asma-Zergui

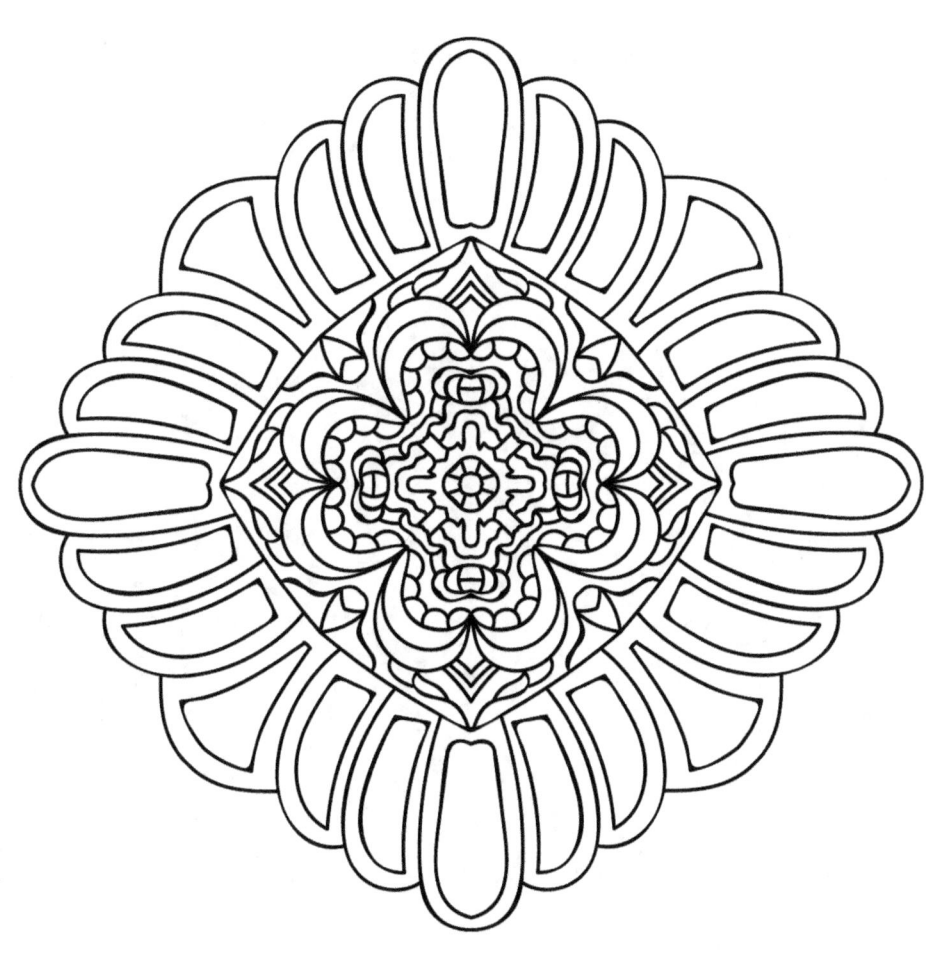

Contributing Artist
T.J.
USA

Facebook : TJsArtCorner

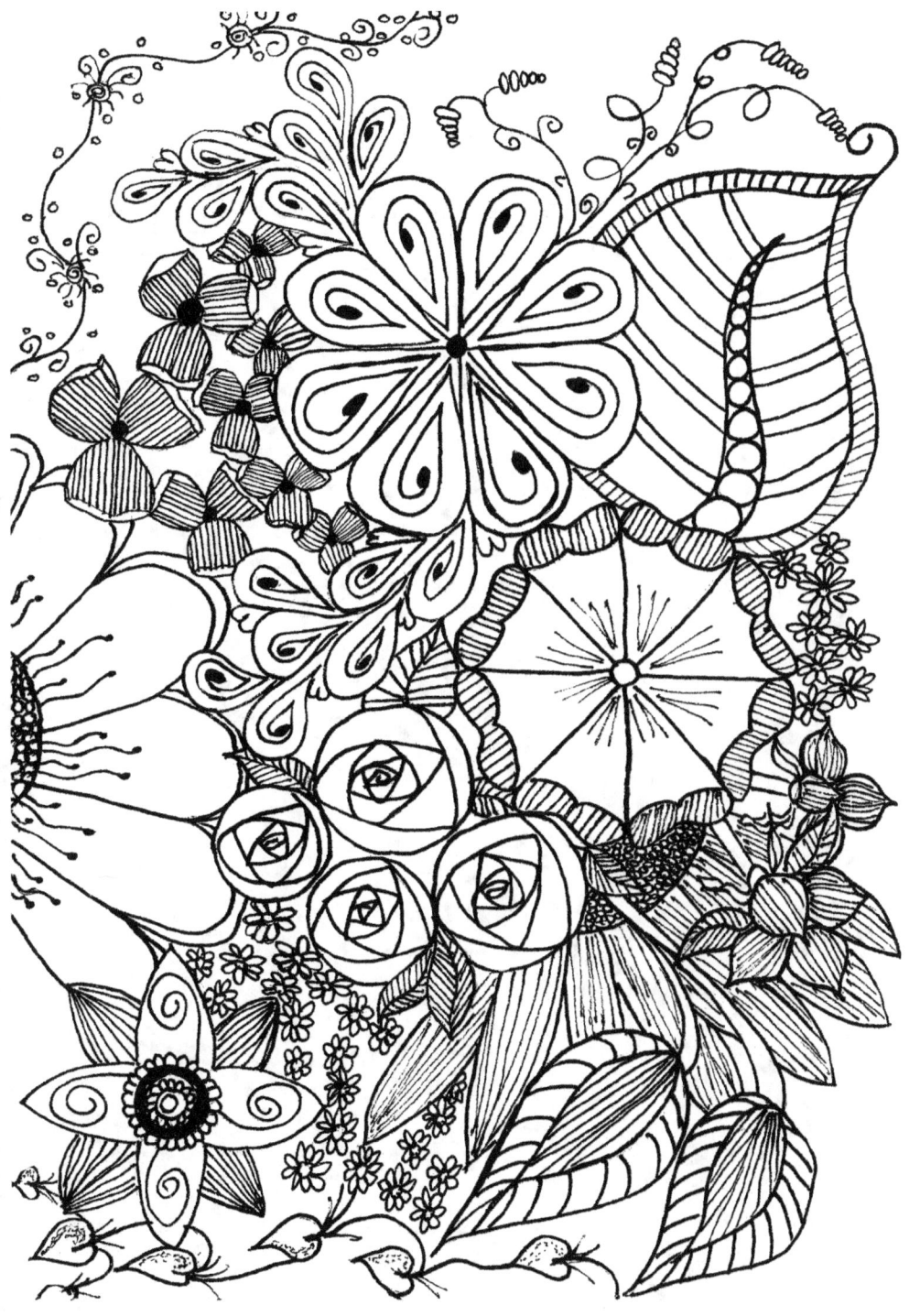

Contributing Artist
T.J.
USA

Facebook : TJsArtCorner

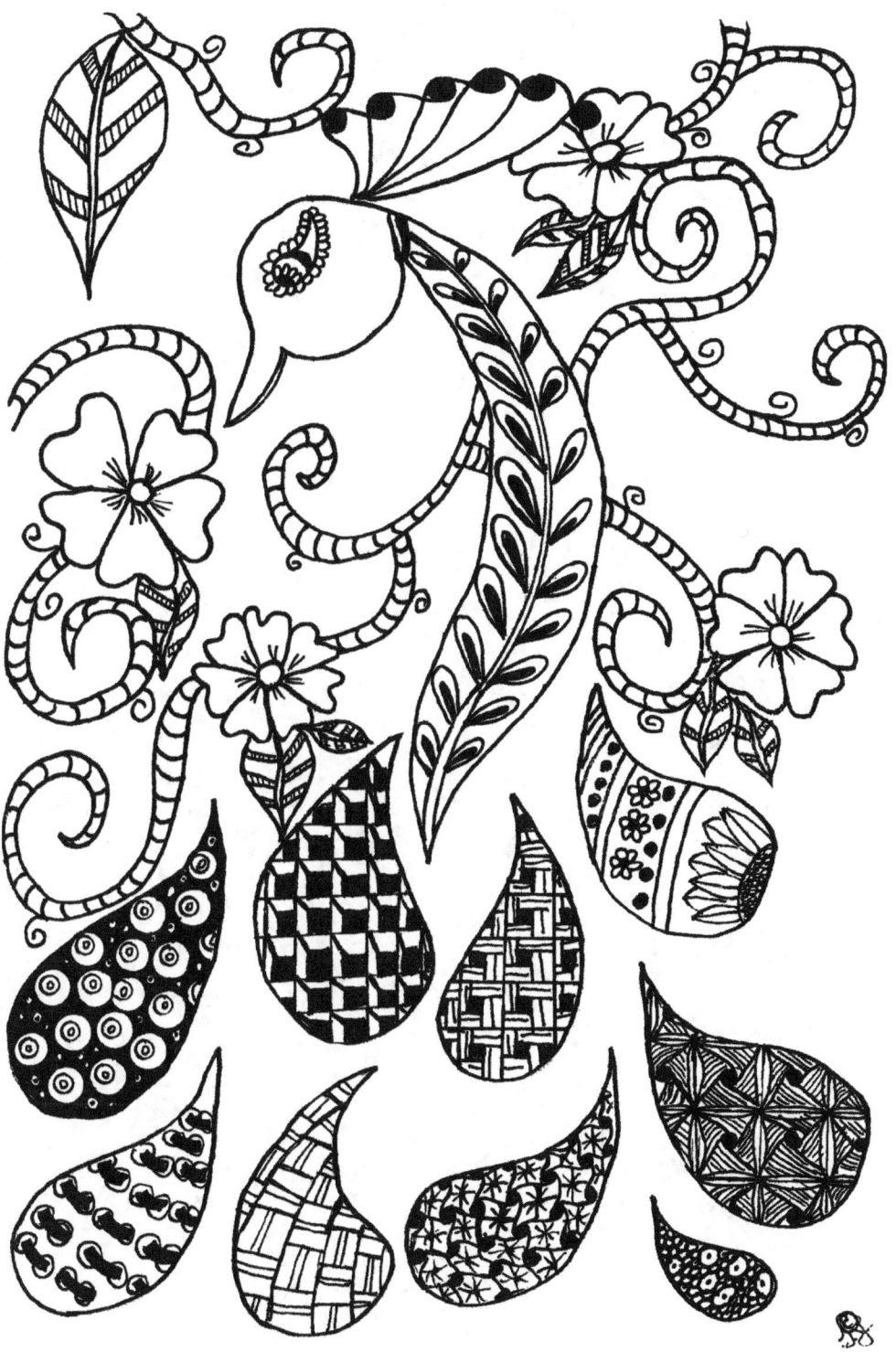

Contributing Artist
T.J.
USA

Facebook : TJsArtCorner

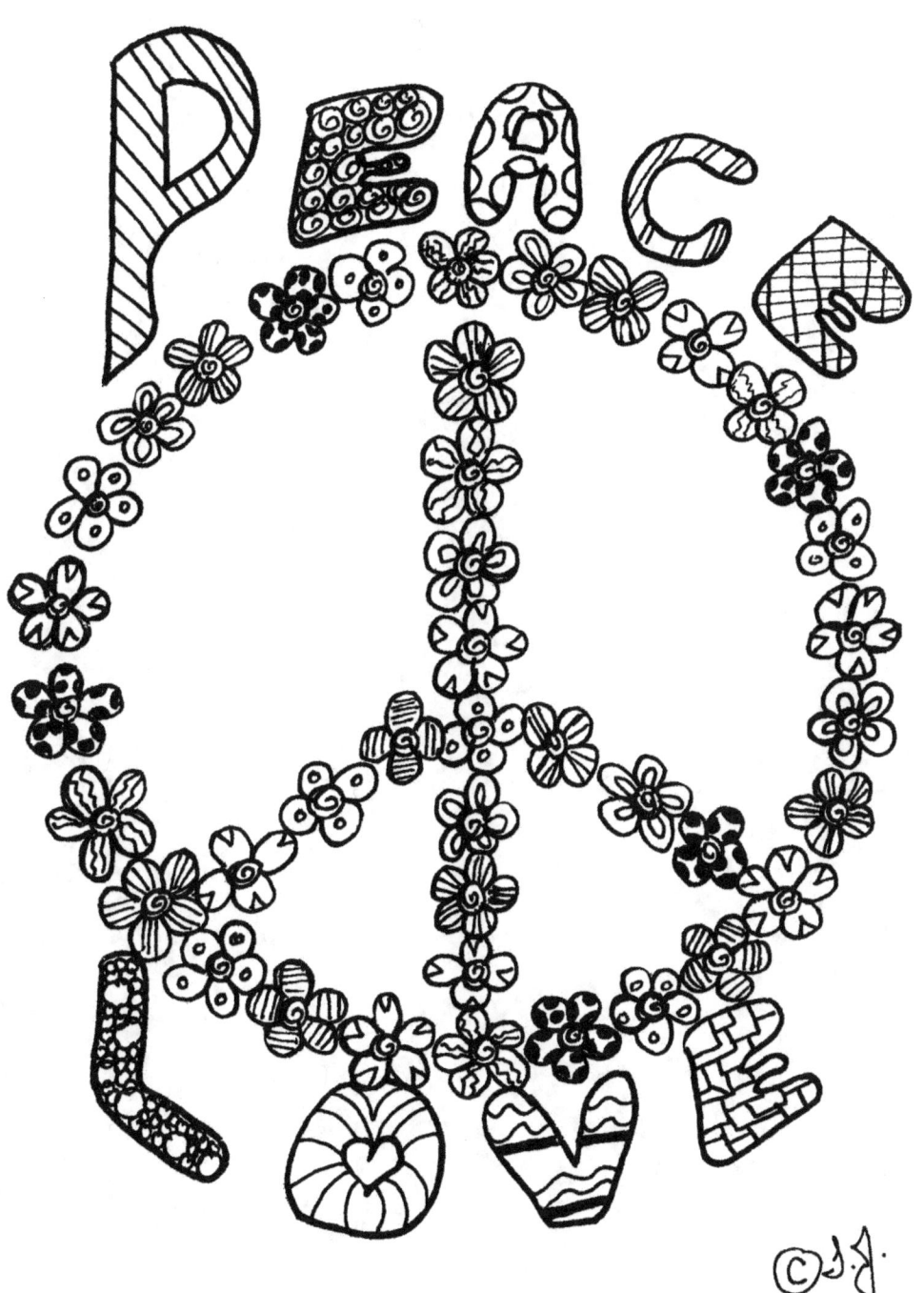

Contributing Artist
T.J.
USA

Facebook : TJsArtCorner

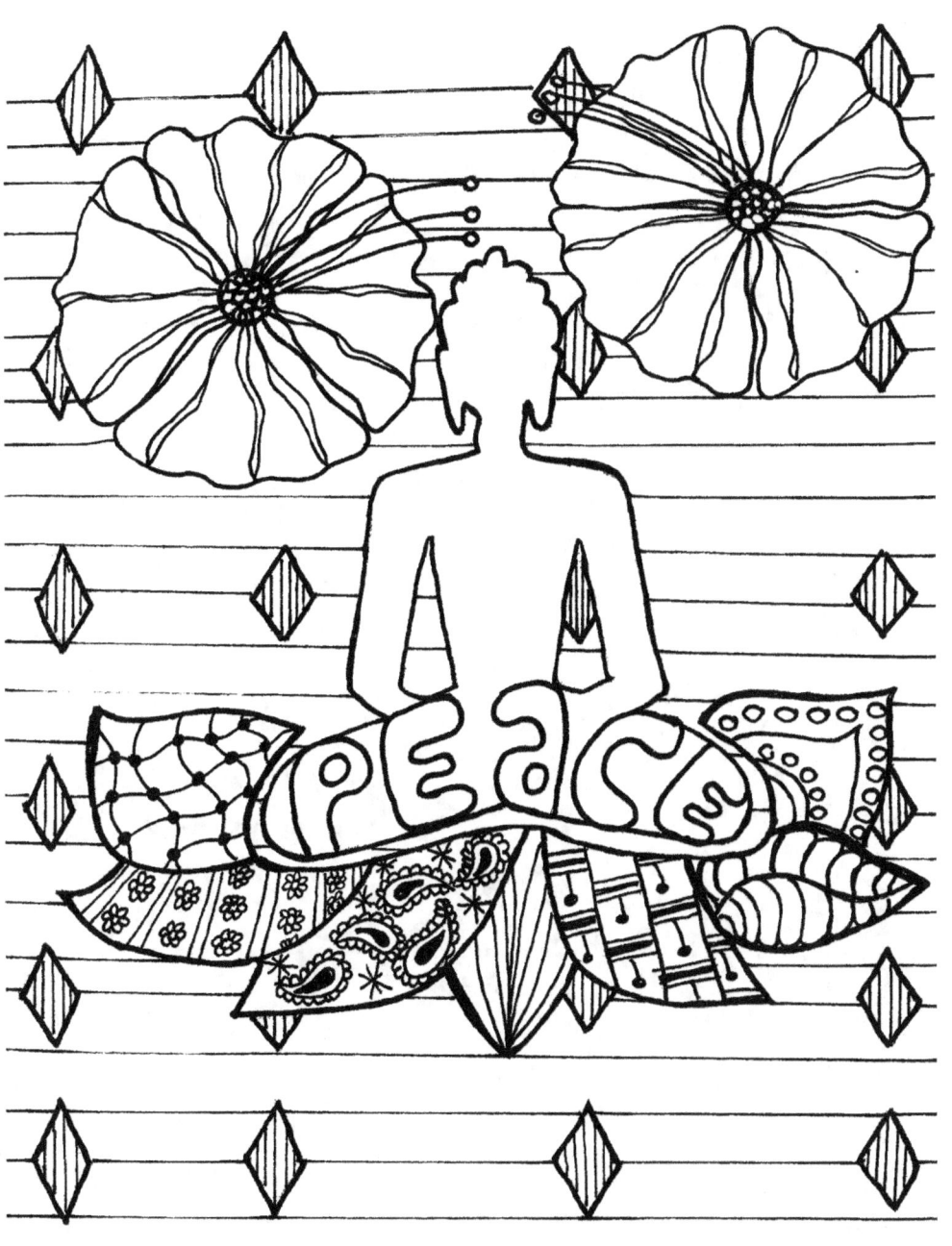

Contributing Artist
T.J.
USA

Facebook : TJsArtCorner

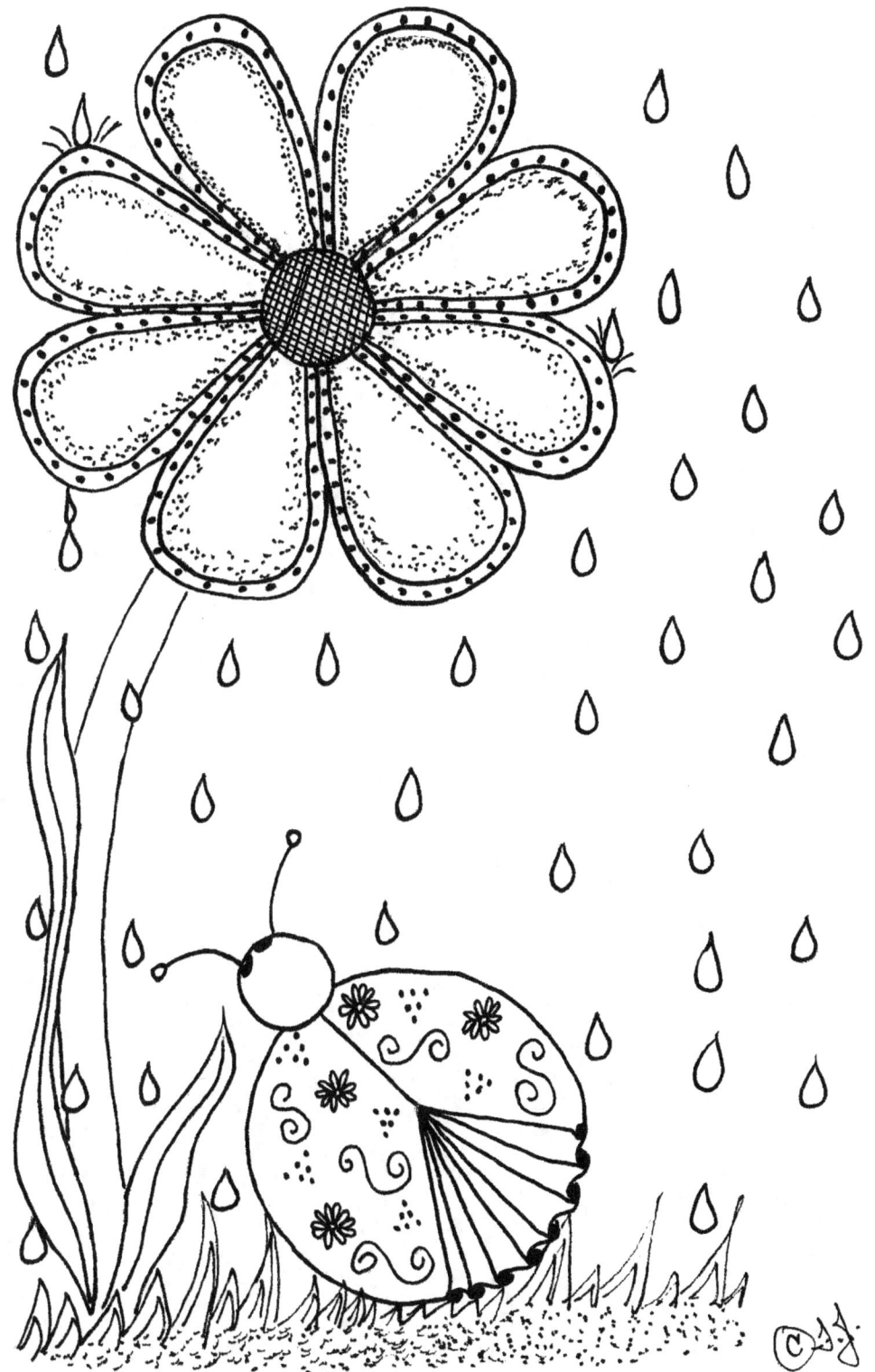

Contributing Artist
Rover Hsiao
Taiwan

Facebook : roverhsiao2015

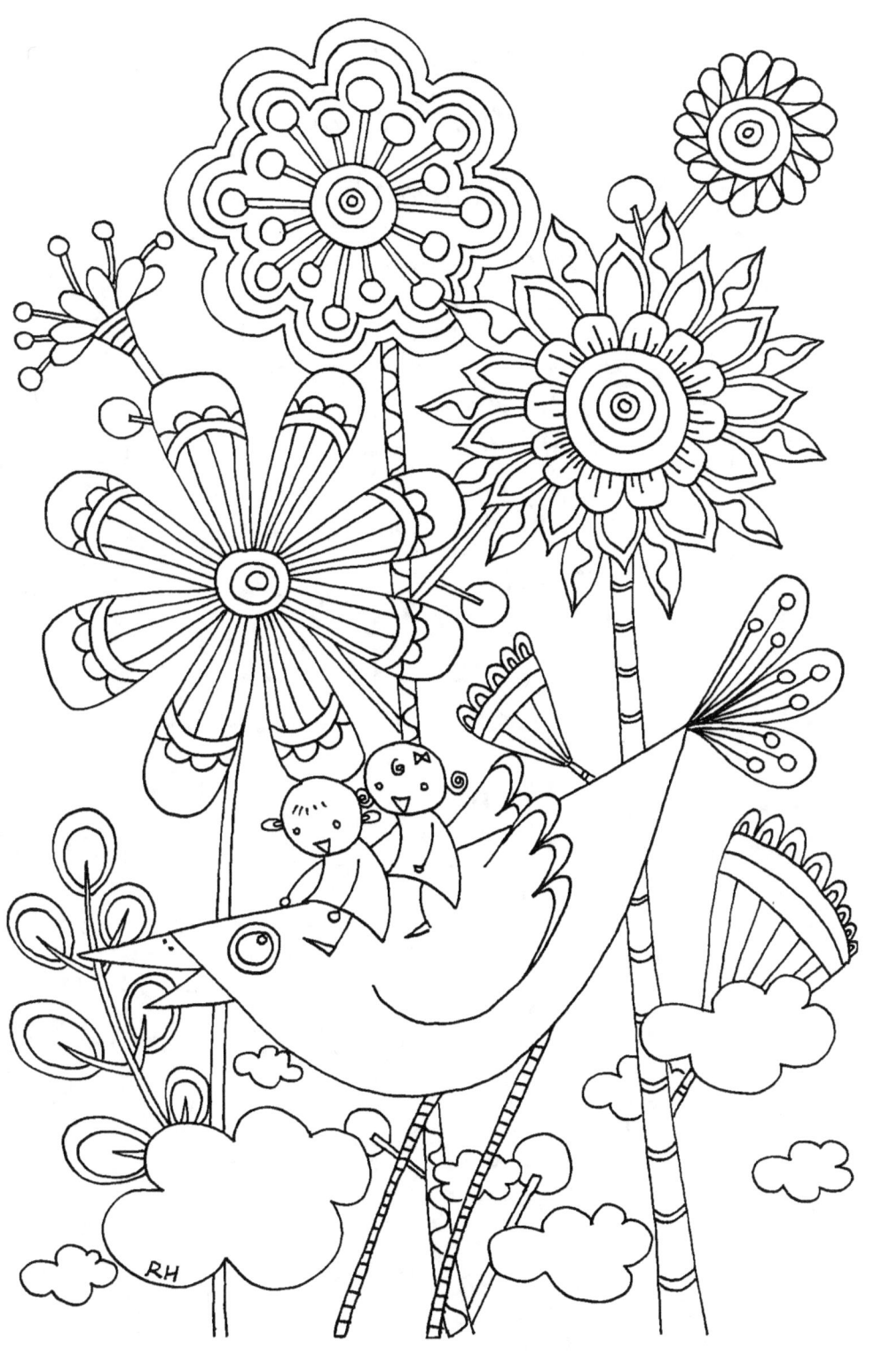

Contributing Artist
Rover Hsiao
Taiwan

Facebook : roverhsiao2015

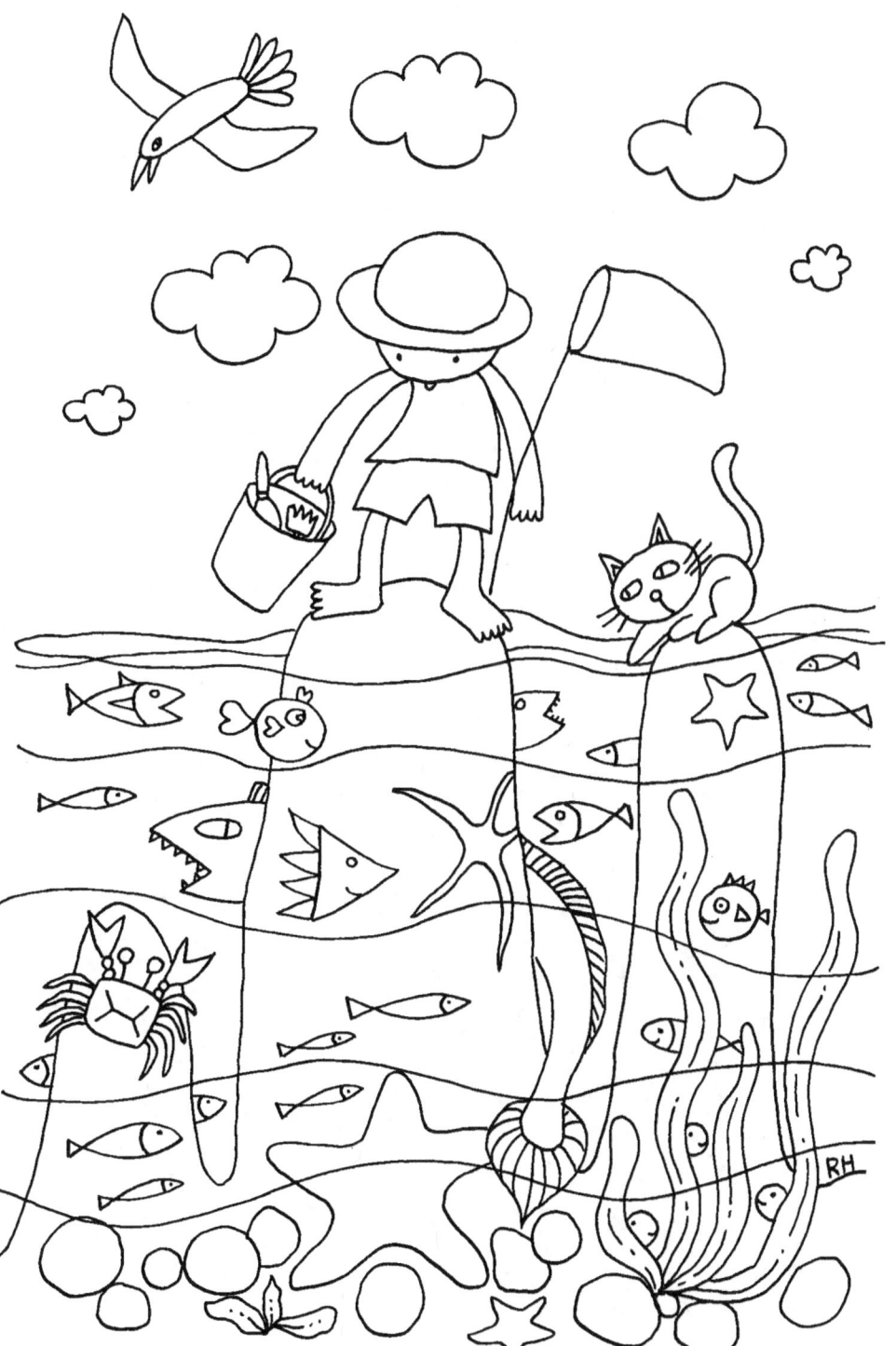

Contributing Artist
Rover Hsiao
Taiwan

Facebook : roverhsiao2015

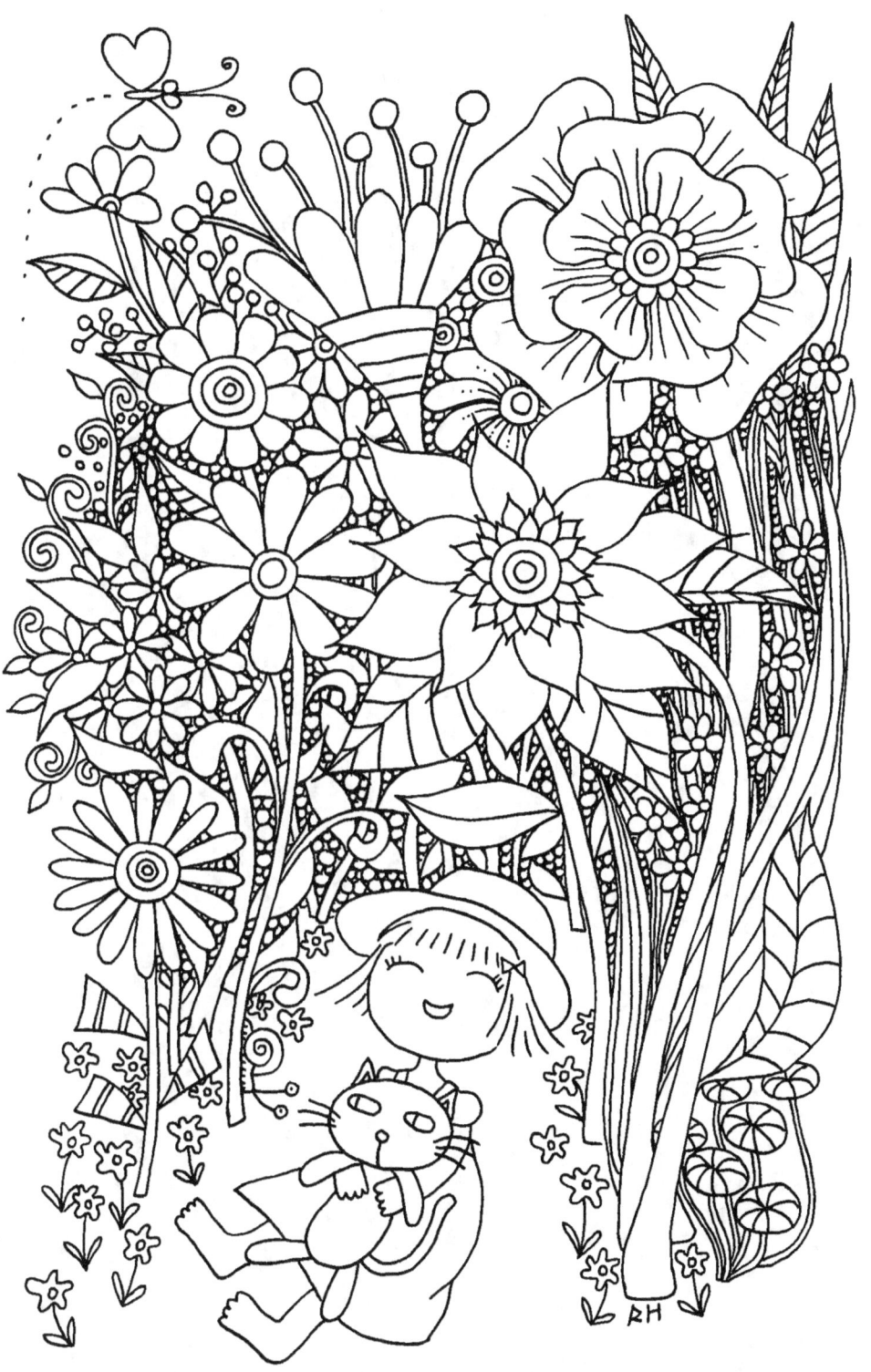

Contributing Artist
Rover Hsiao
Taiwan

Facebook : roverhsiao2015

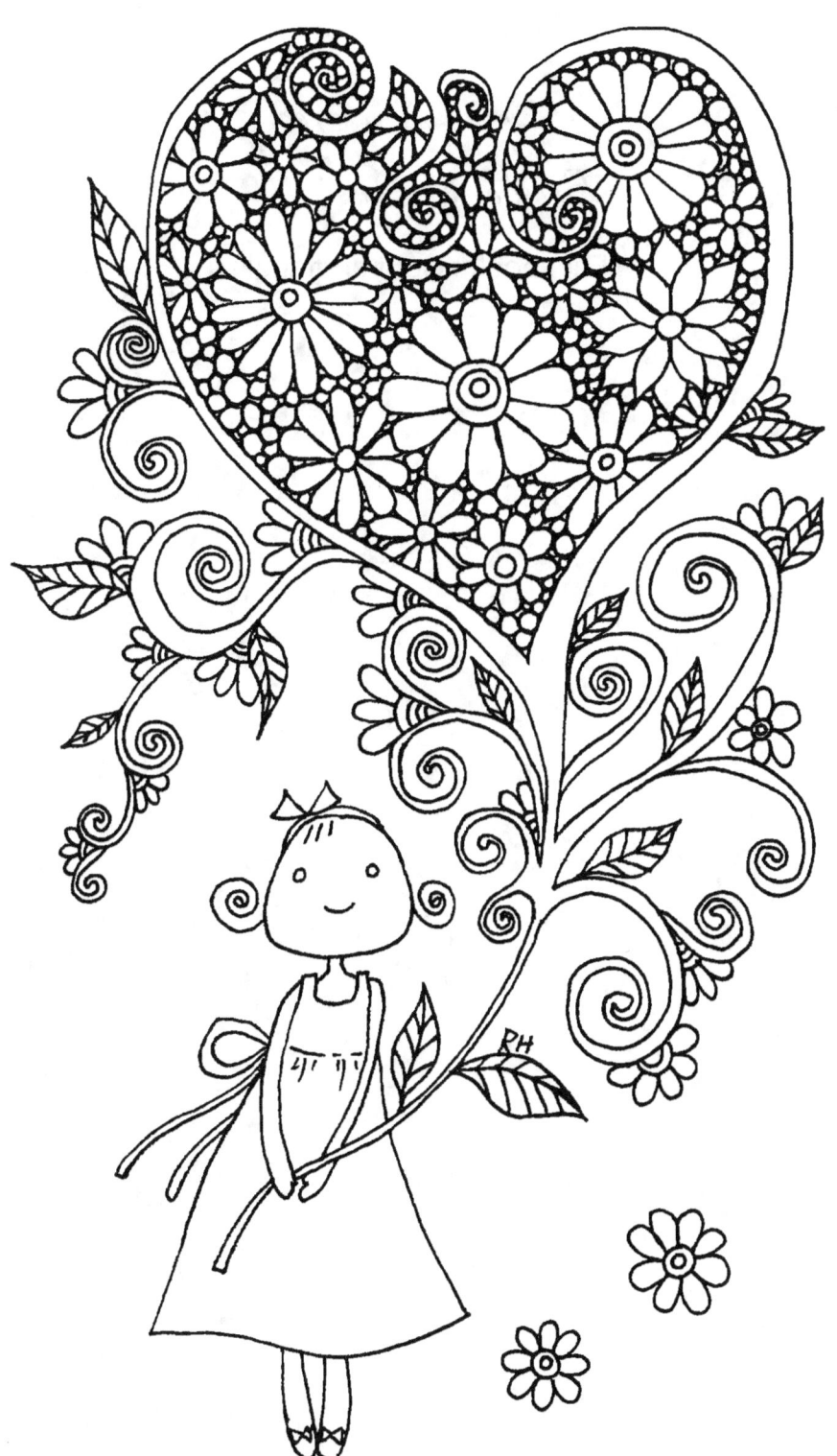

Contributing Artist
Lynne McGee
Brisbane, Australia

Facebook : Colorandtangle

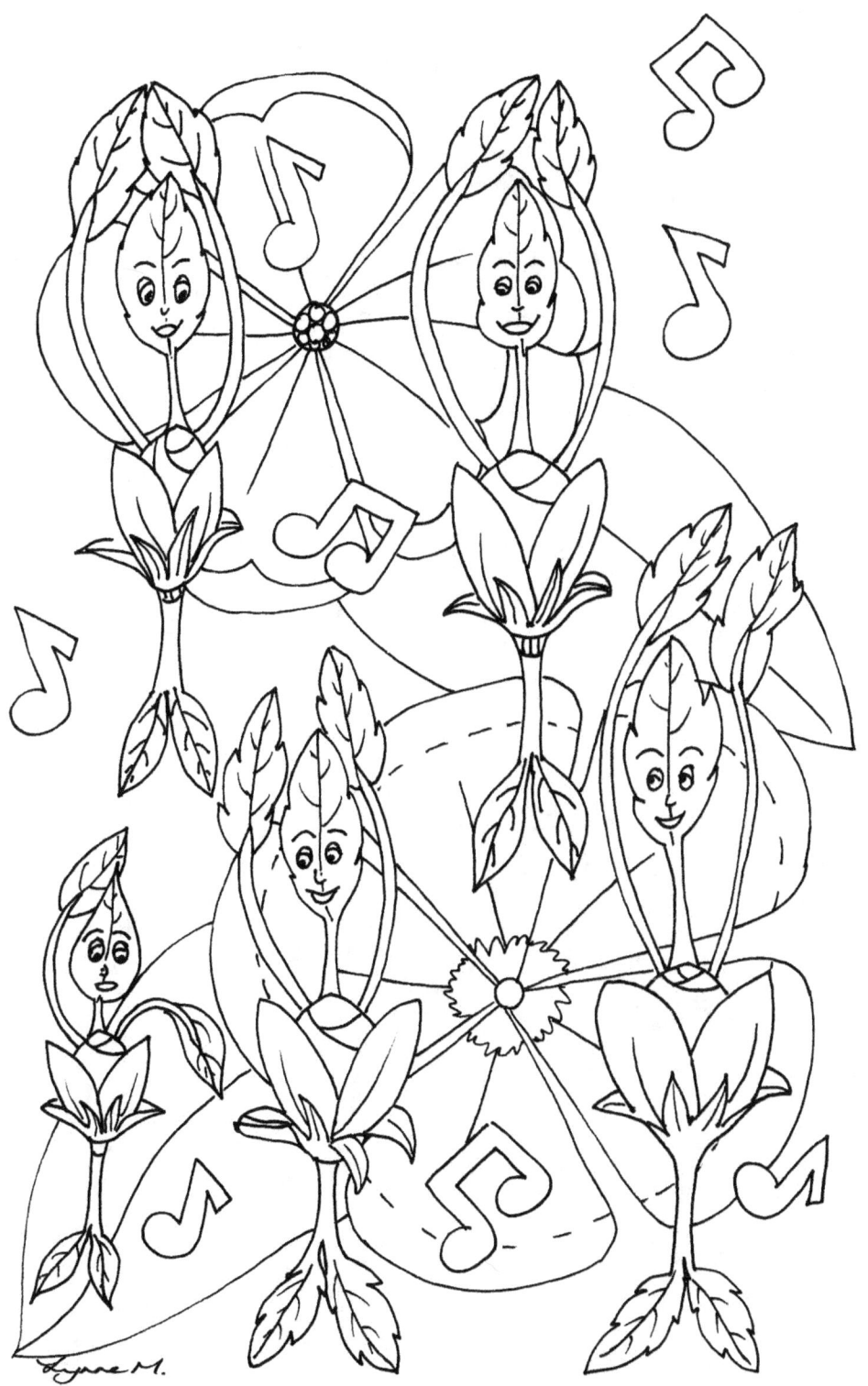

Contributing Artist
Lynne McGee
Brisbane, Australia

Facebook : Colorandtangle

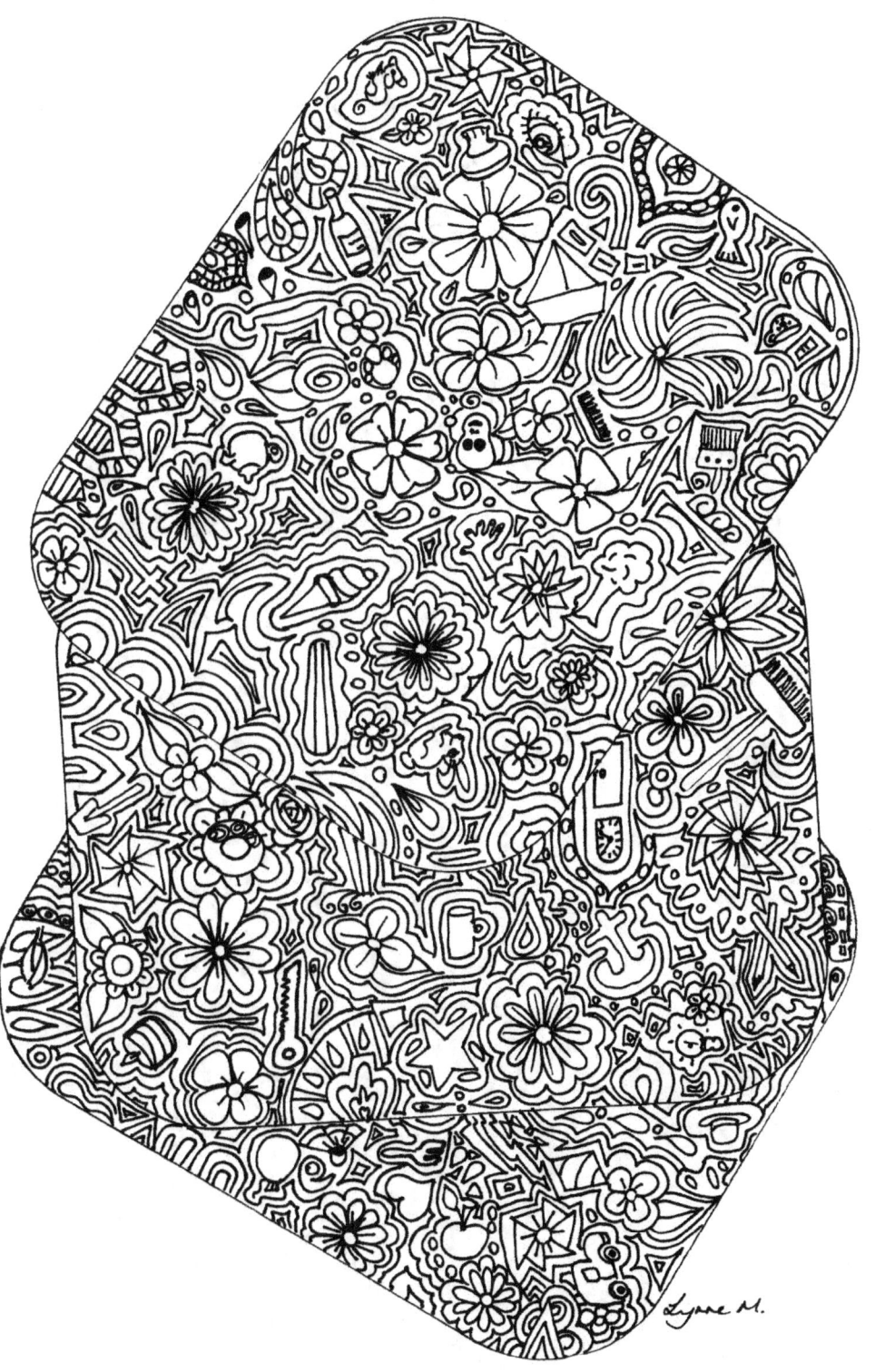

Contributing Artist
Lynne McGee
Brisbane, Australia

Facebook : Colorandtangle

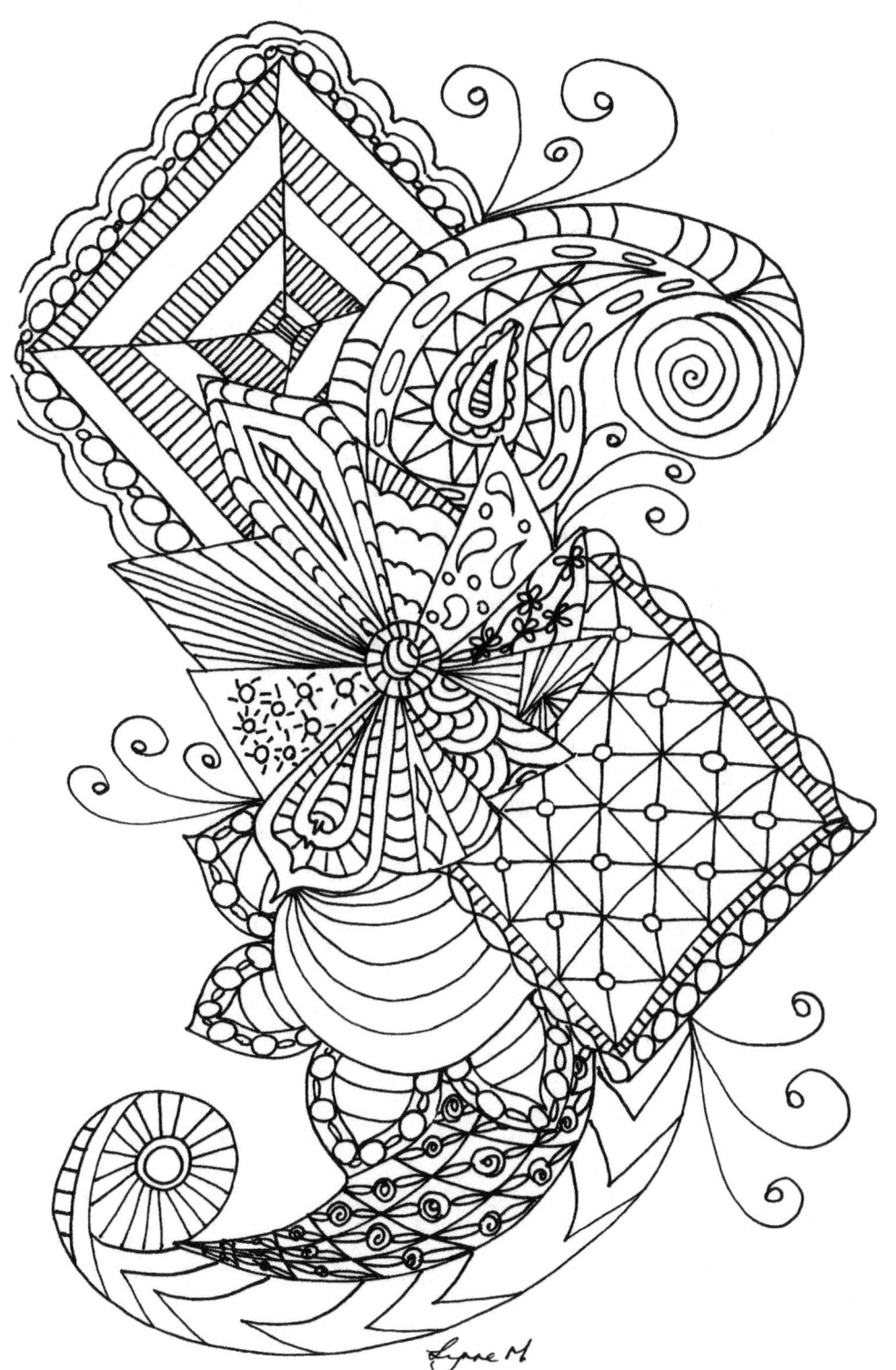

Contributing Artist
Lynne McGee
Brisbane, Australia

Facebook : Colorandtangle

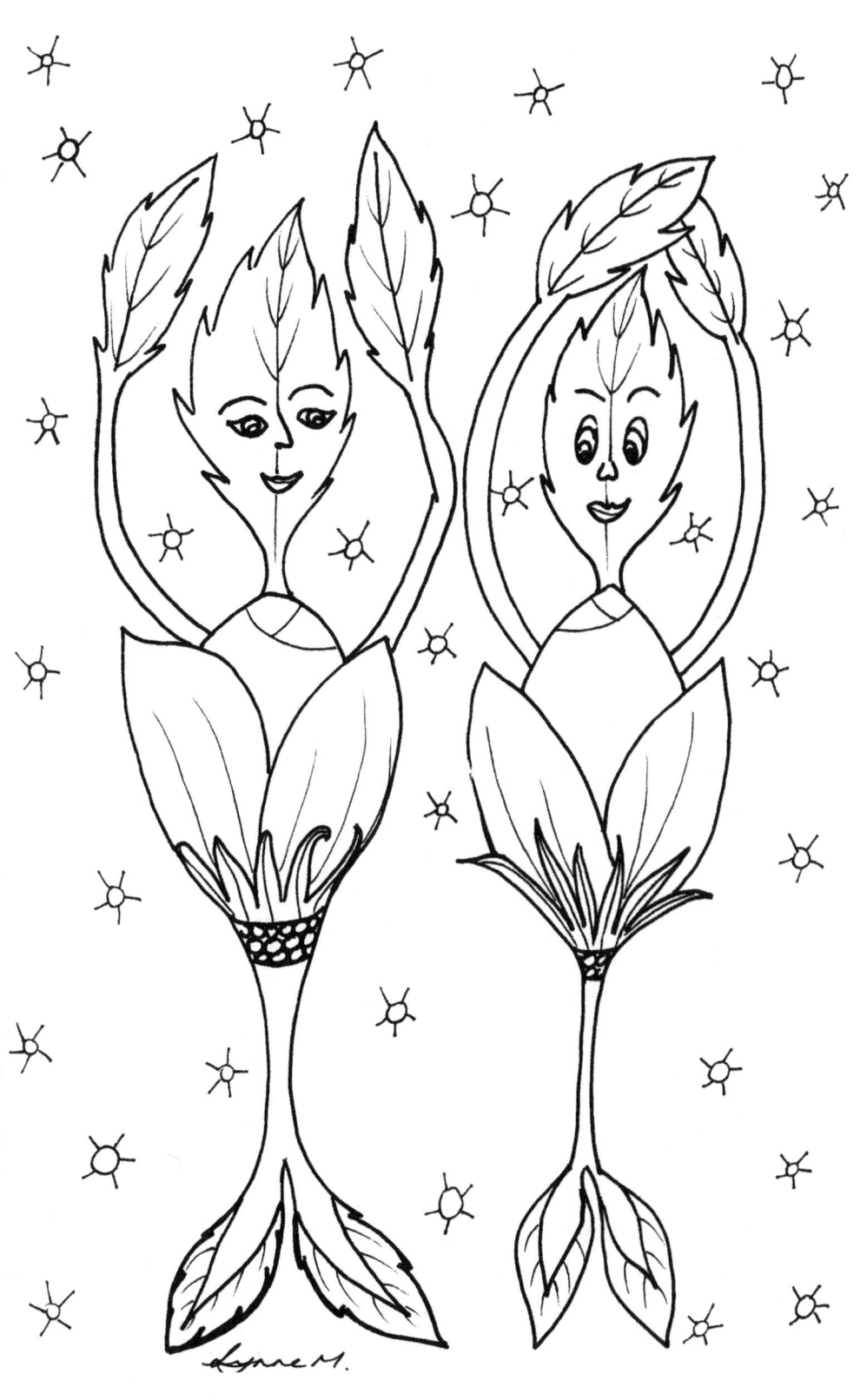

Contributing Artist
Laurie Beauchamp
USA

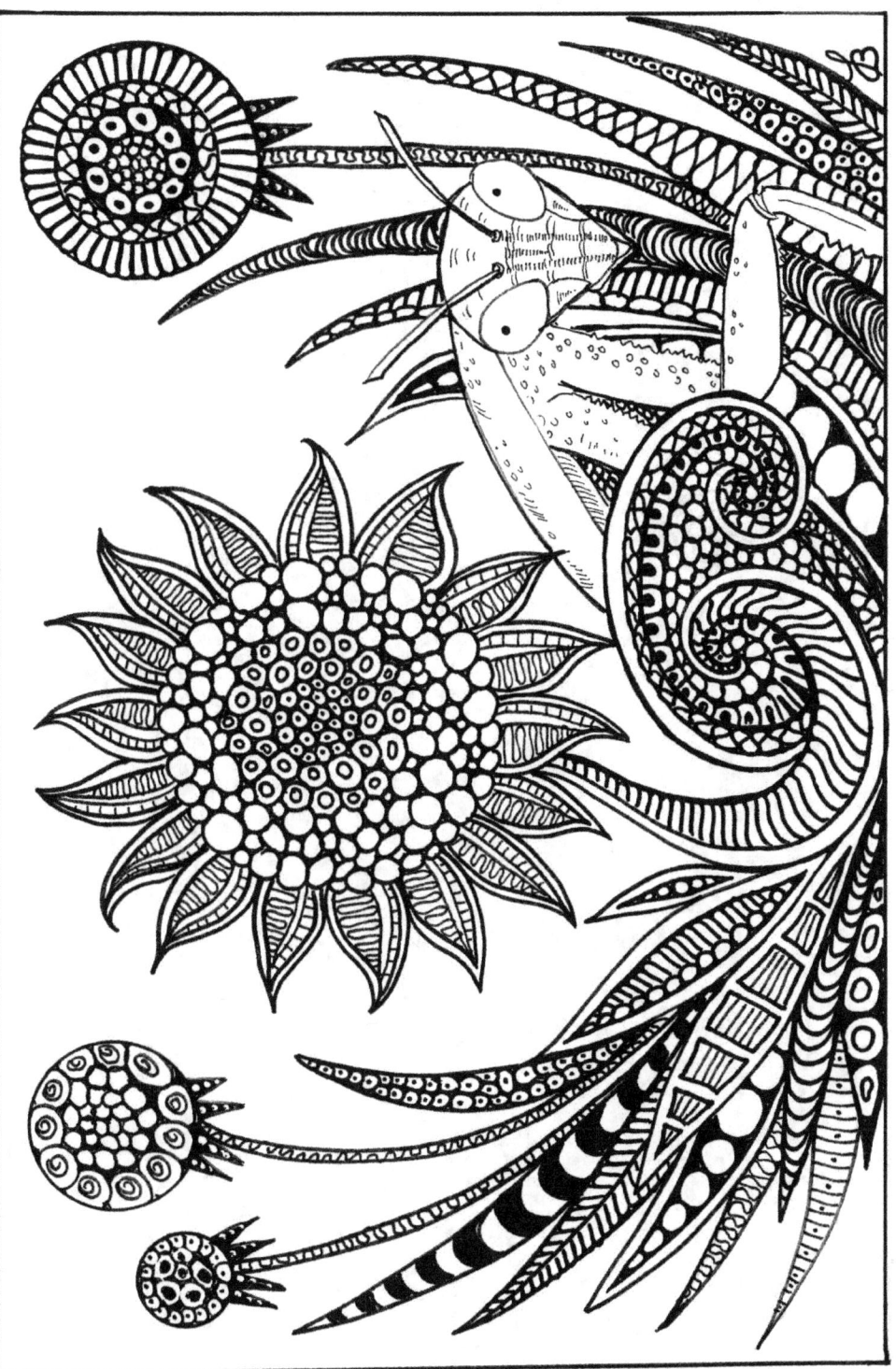

Contributing Artist
Laurie Beauchamp
USA

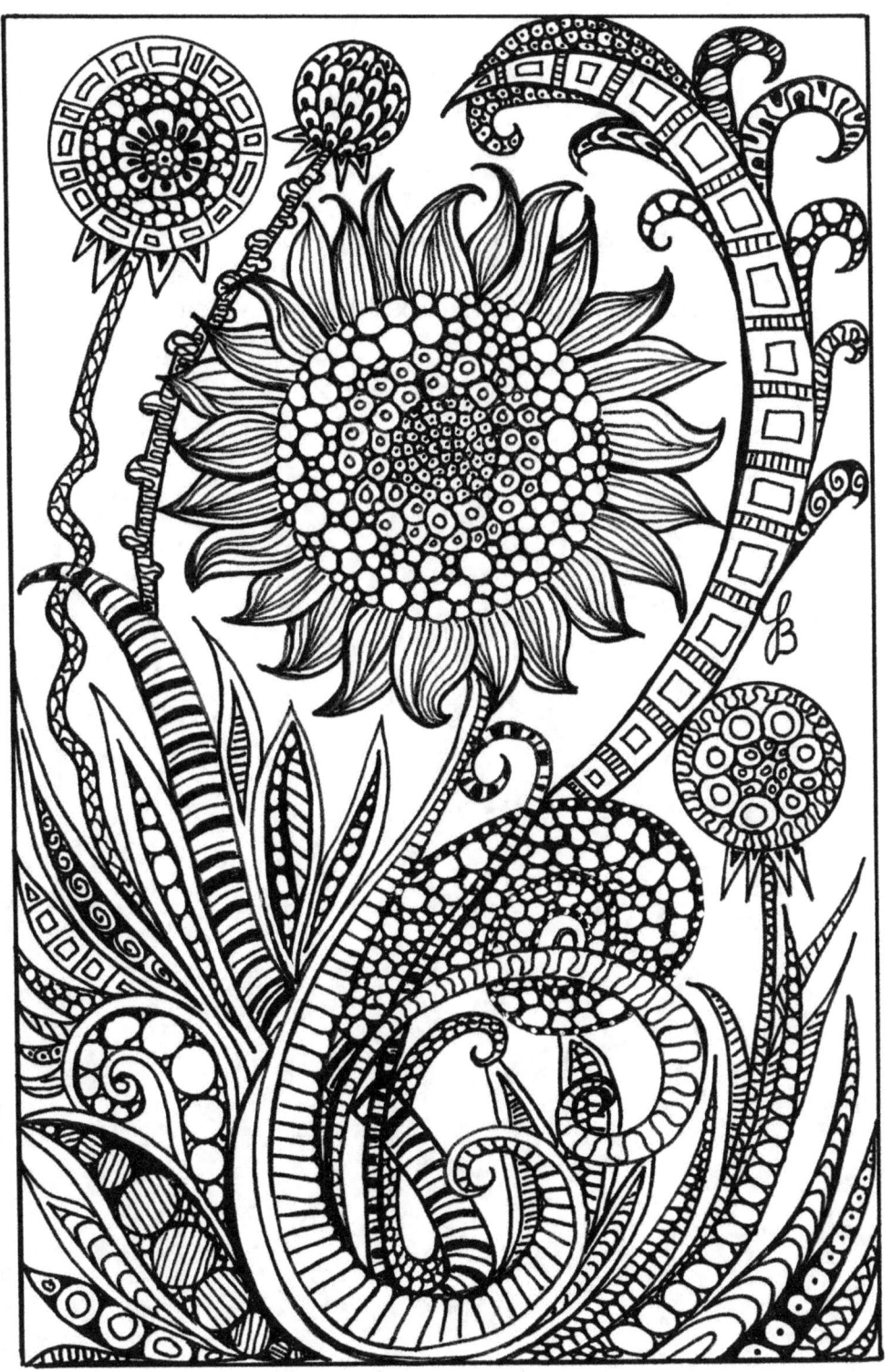

Contributing Artist
MWMS-Johanna Ans
The Netherlands

Blog : mywaymystylejohannaans.wordpress.com

Facebook : Johanna-Ans-My-creative-site

Contributing Artist
MWMS-Johanna Ans
The Netherlands

Blog : mywaymystylejohannaans.wordpress.com

Facebook : Johanna-Ans-My-creative-site

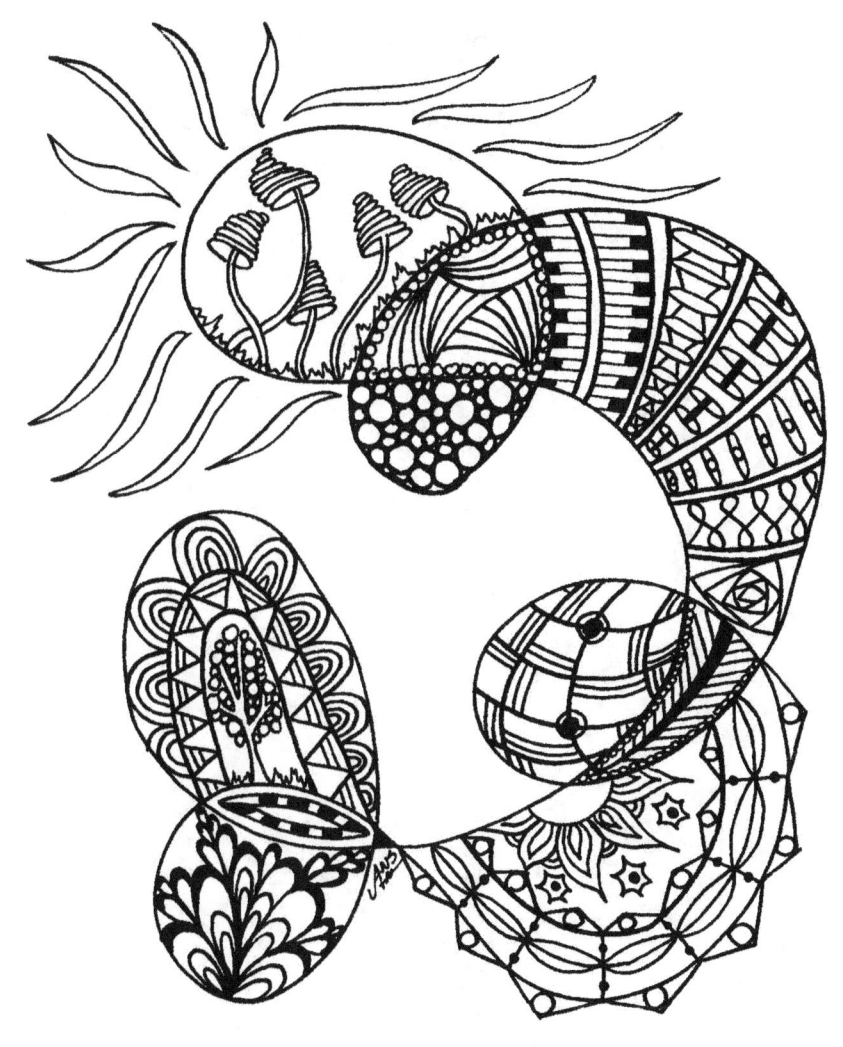

Contributing Artist
MWMS-Johanna Ans
The Netherlands

Blog : mywaymystylejohannaans.wordpress.com

Facebook : Johanna-Ans-My-creative-site

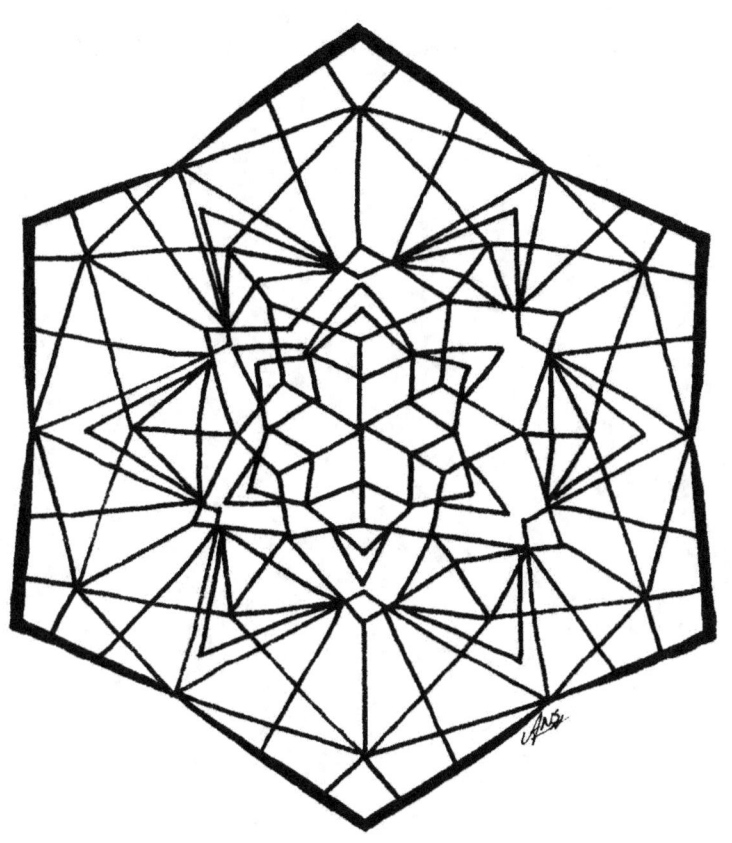

Contributing Artist
MWMS-Johanna Ans
The Netherlands

Blog : mywaymystylejohannaans.wordpress.com

Facebook : Johanna-Ans-My-creative-site

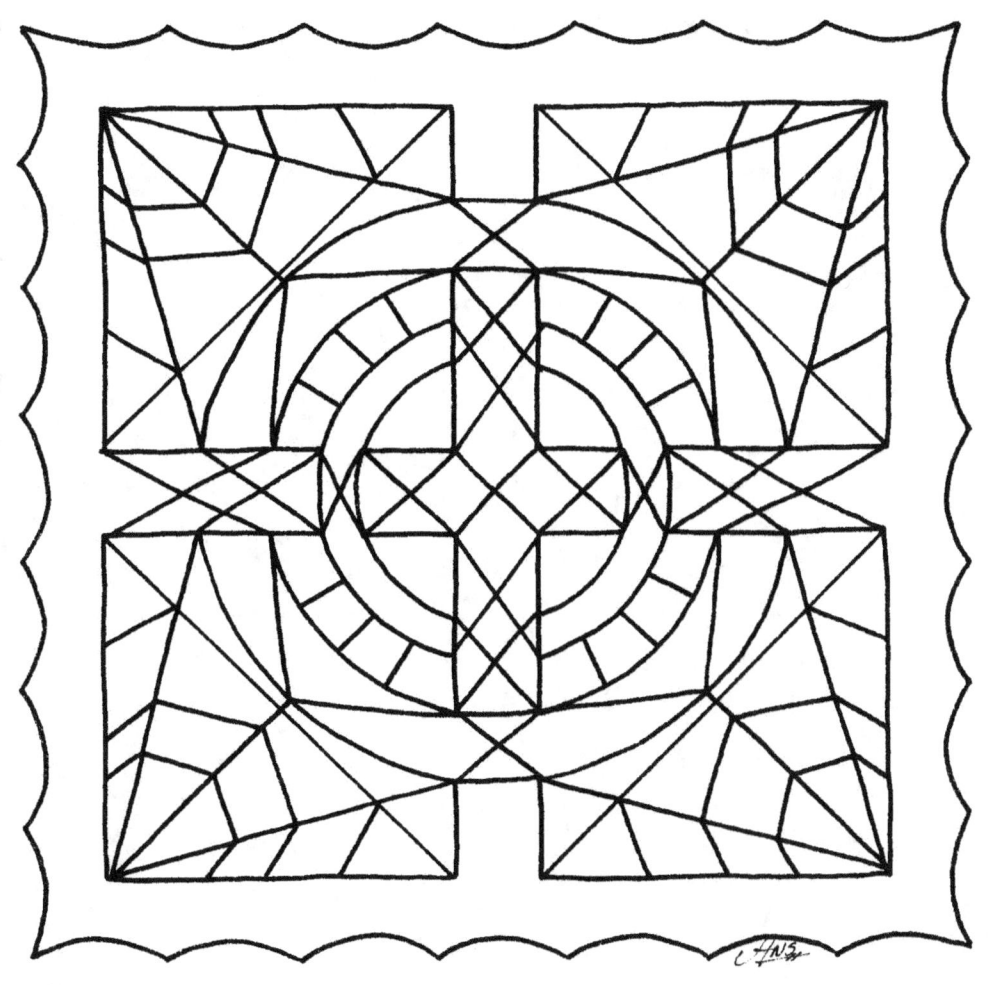

Contributing Artist
MWMS-Johanna Ans
The Netherlands

Blog : mywaymystylejohannaans.wordpress.com

Facebook : Johanna-Ans-My-creative-site

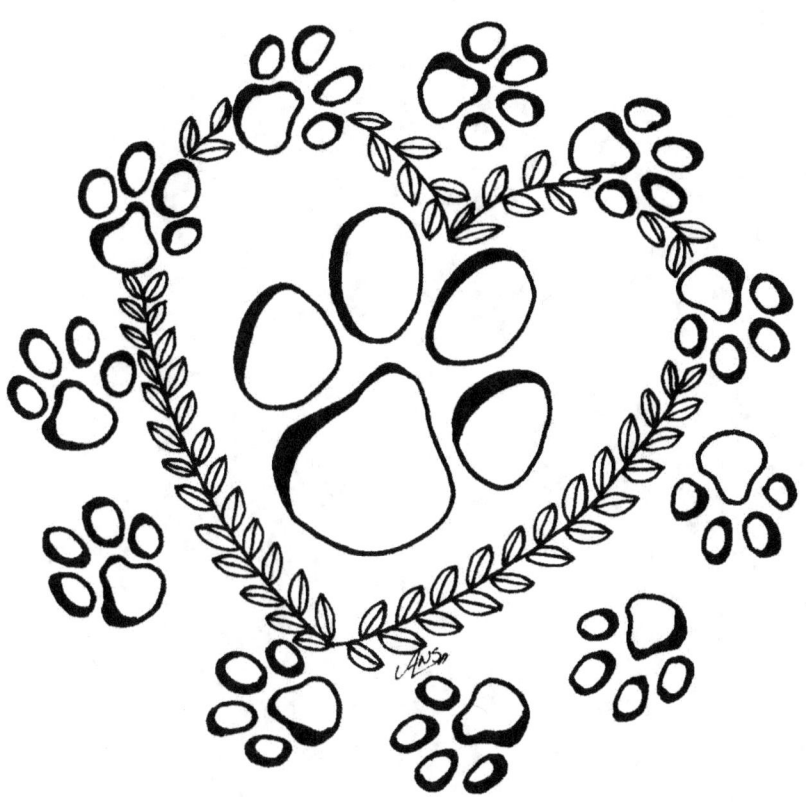

Contributing Artist
Jenny Wei
Taiwan

Facebook : zentanglefun

Contributing Artist
Jenny Wei
Taiwan

Facebook : zentanglefun

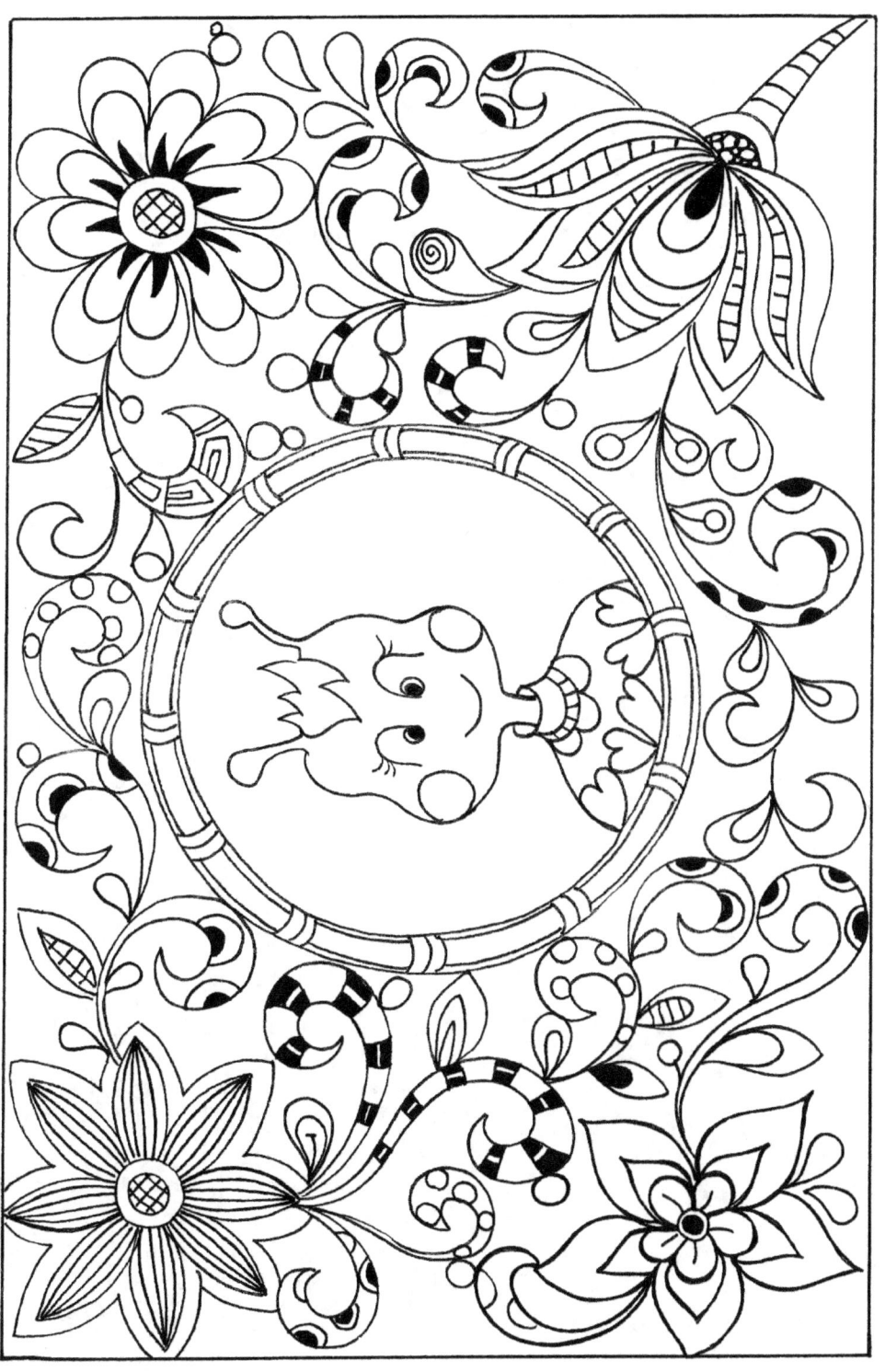

Contributing Artist
Jenny Wei
Taiwan

Facebook : zentanglefun

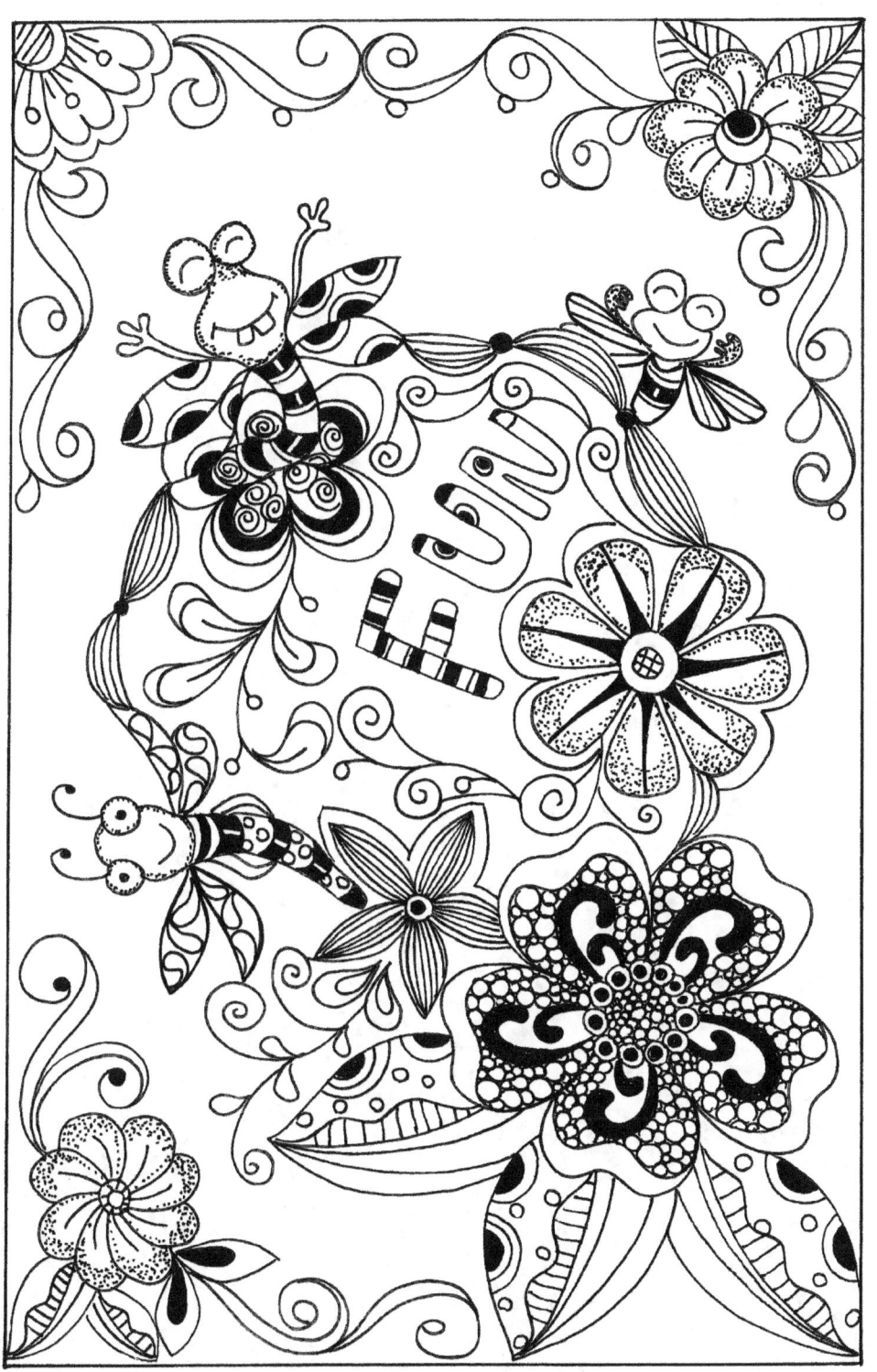

Contributing Artist
Jenny Wei
Taiwan

Facebook : zentanglefun

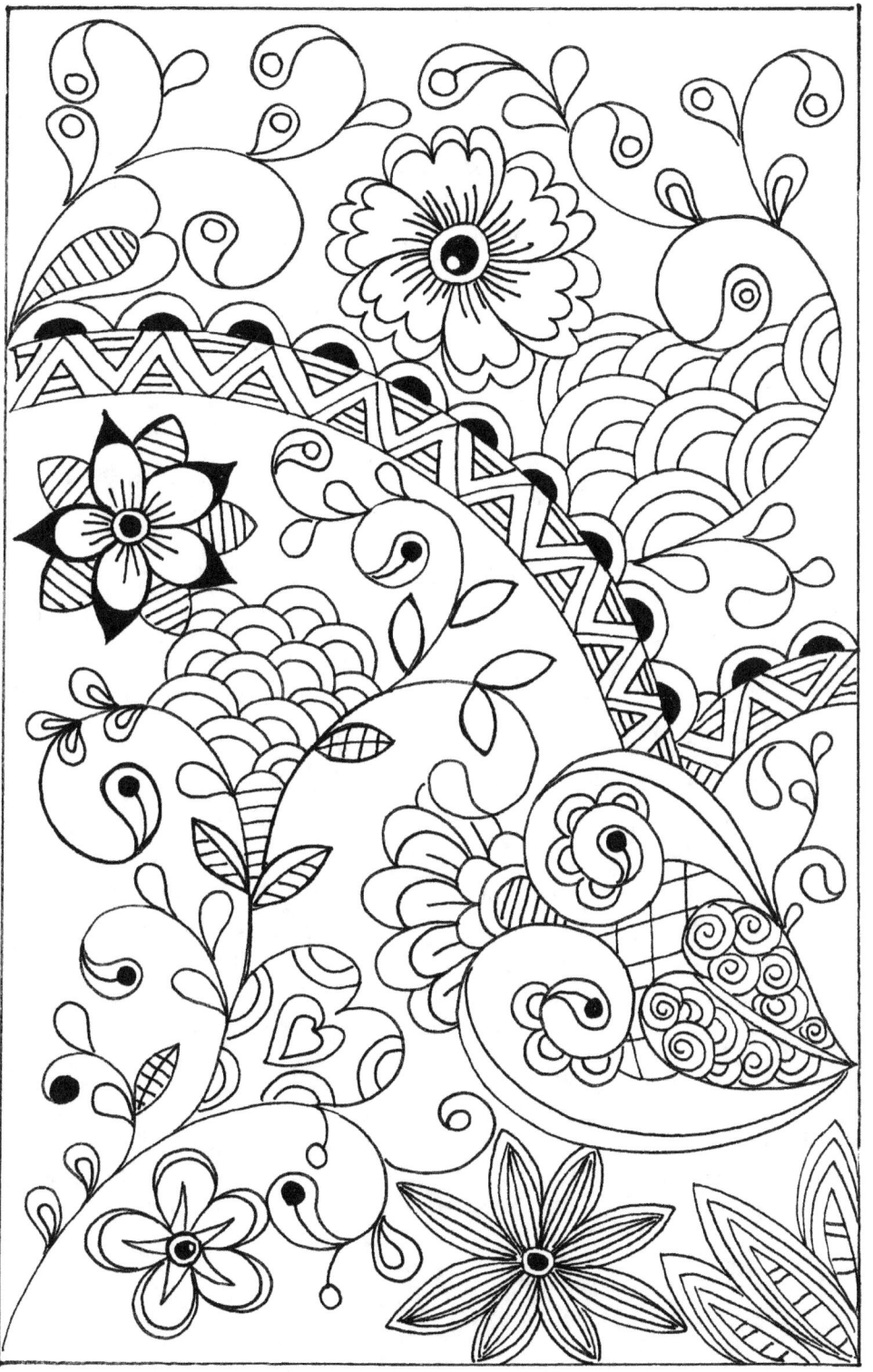

Contributing Artist
Jane Levi
France

Facebook : Cheeky-Cats

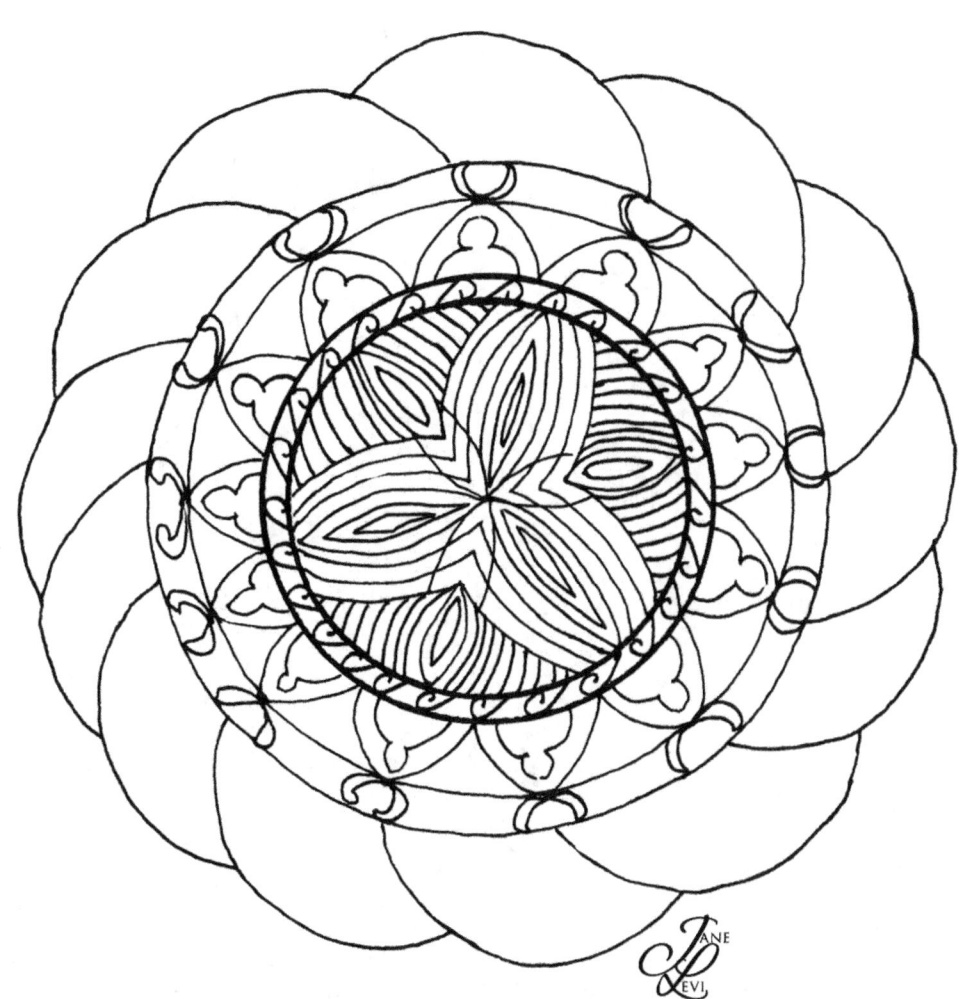

Contributing Artist
Jane Levi
France

Facebook : Cheeky-Cats

Contributing Artist
Yaya
France

Facebook : Les-gribouillis-de-yaya-georgia-merino

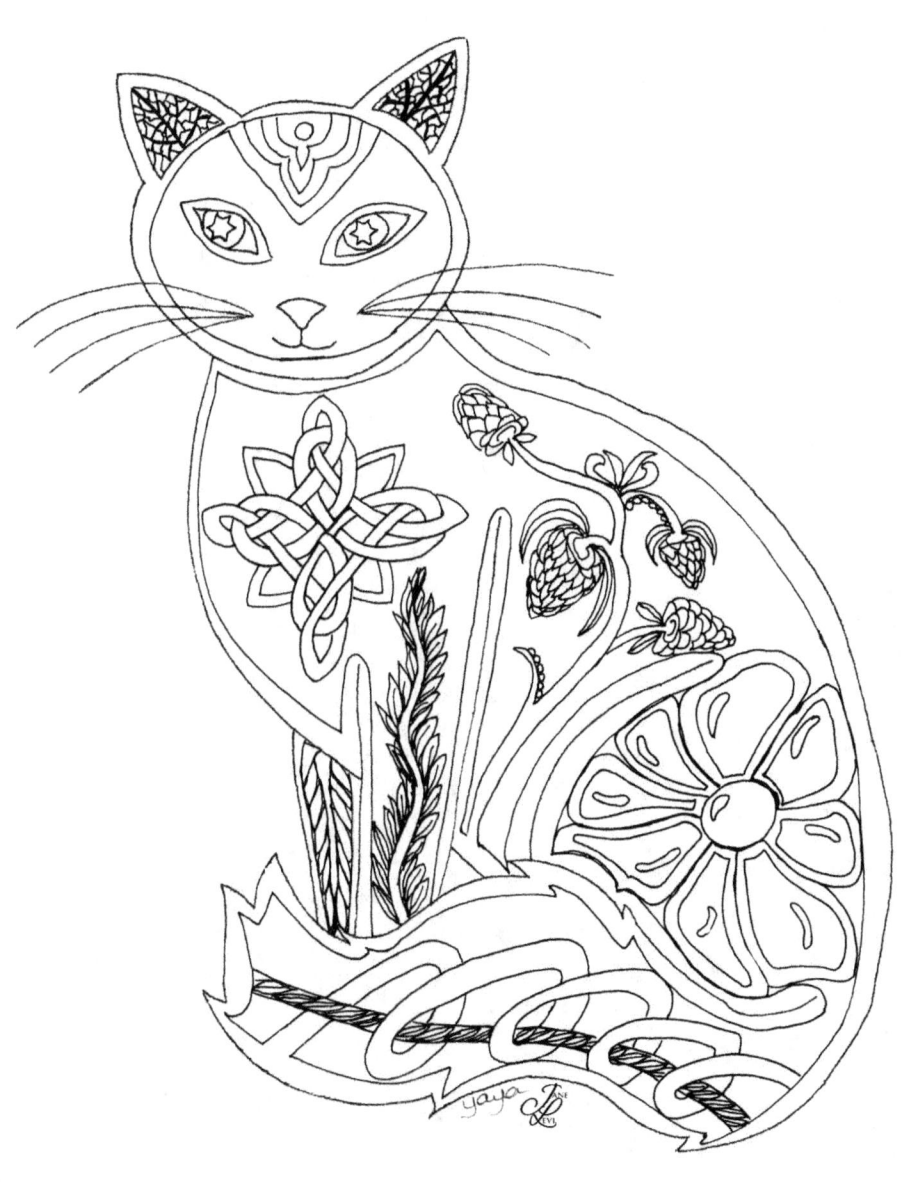

Contributing Artist
Yaya
France

Facebook : Les-gribouillis-de-yaya-georgia-merino

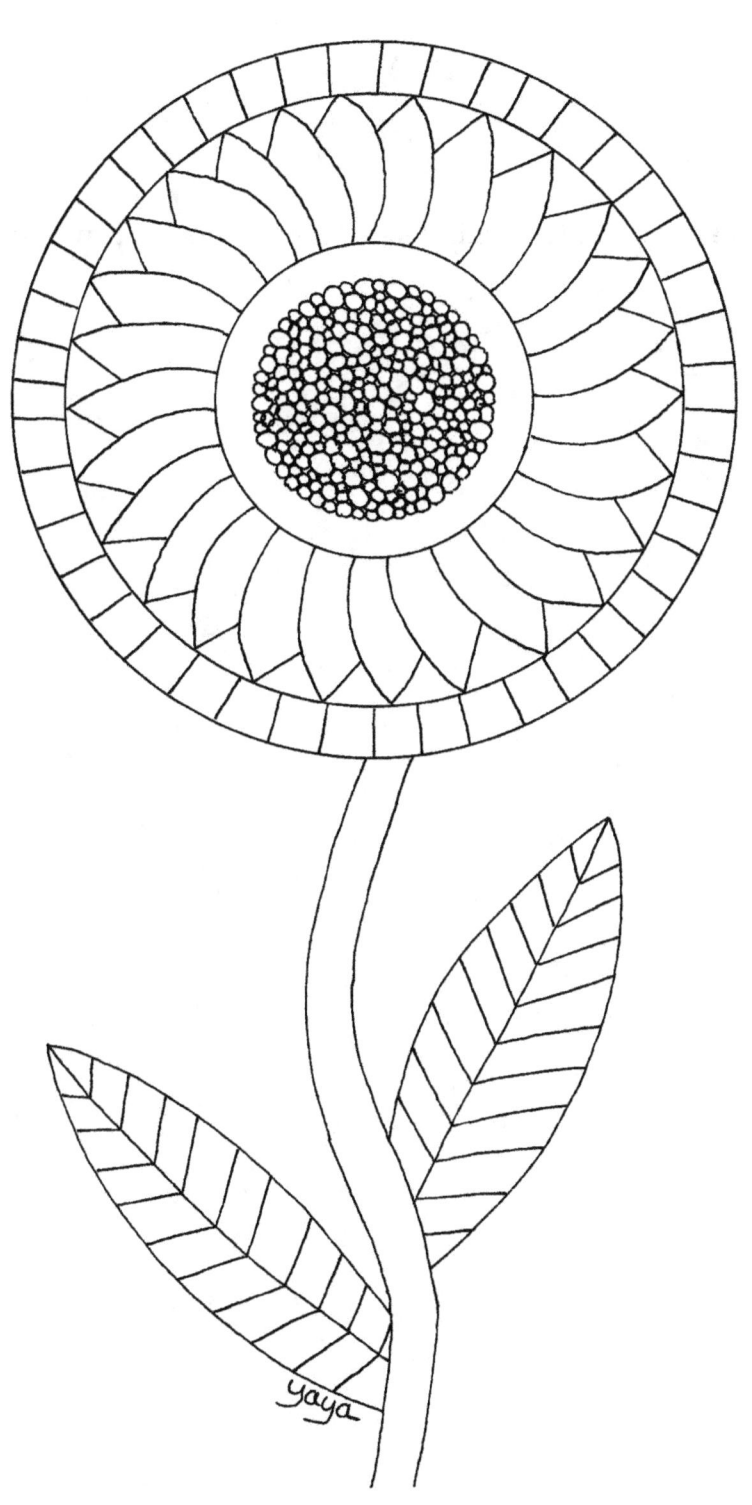

Contributing Artist
Yaya
France

Facebook : Les-gribouillis-de-yaya-georgia-merino

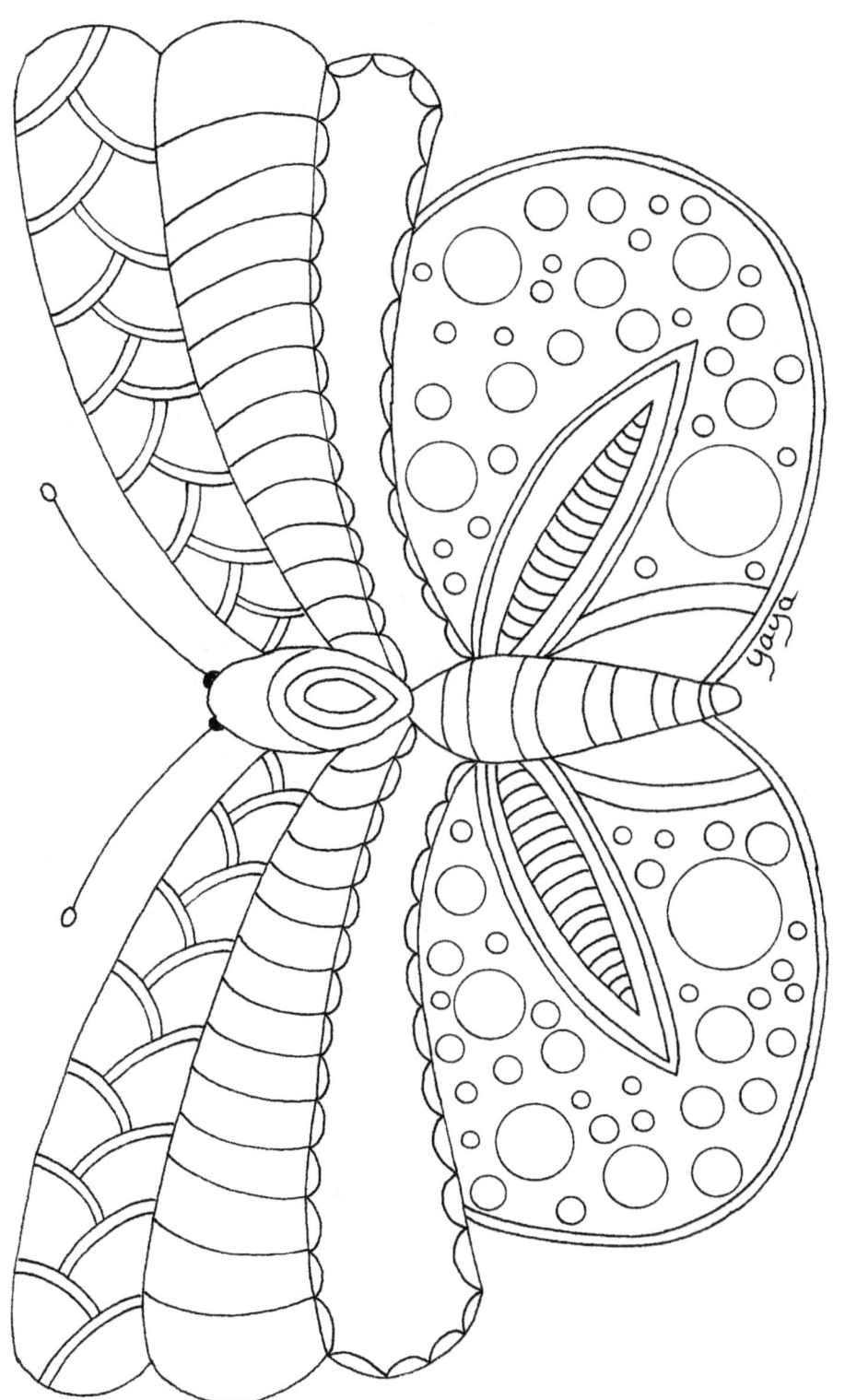

Contributing Artist
Iben Lykke Højholdt
Denmark

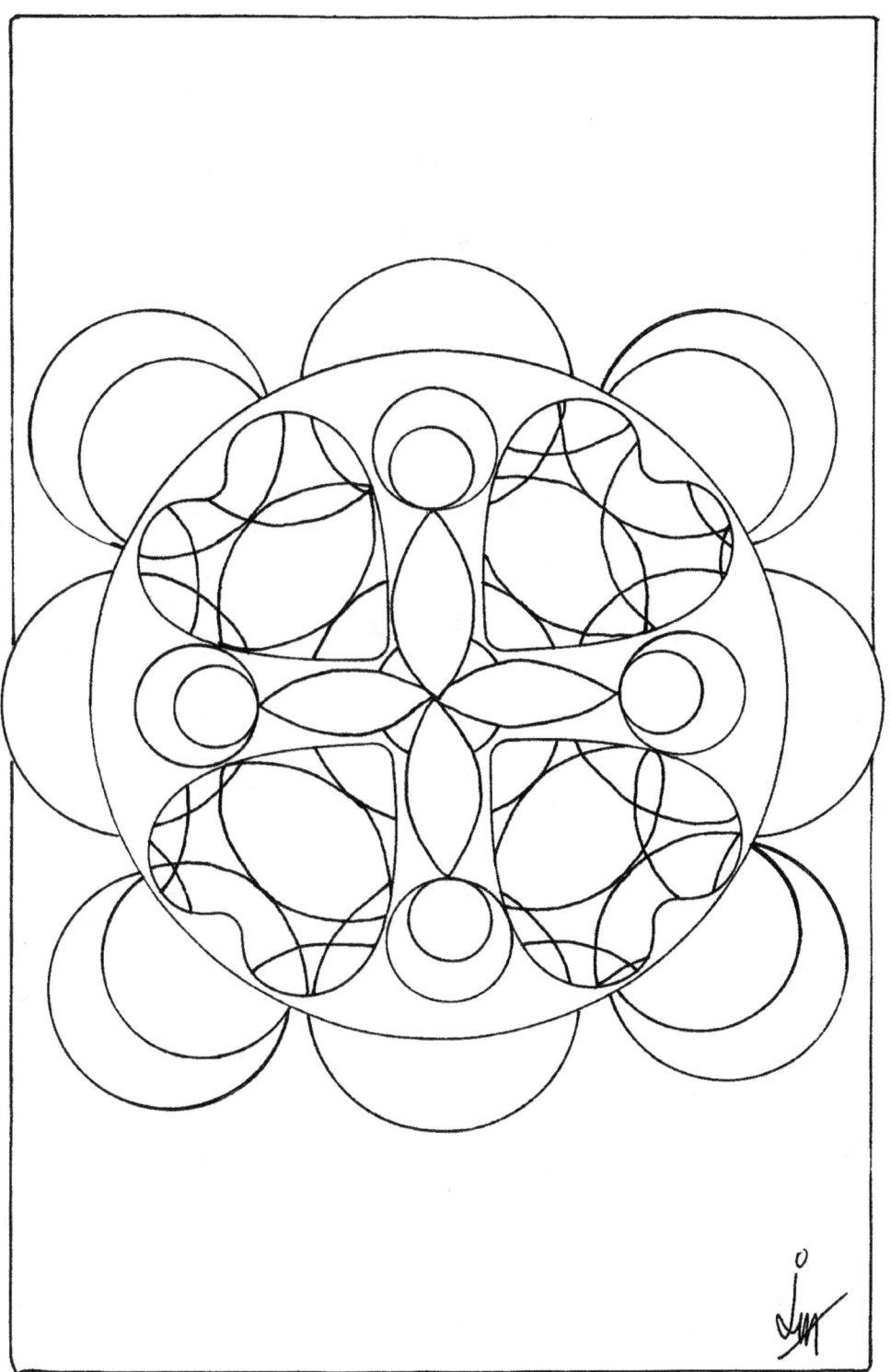

Contributing Artist
Creative Rosalien
Norway

Facebook : Creative Rosalien

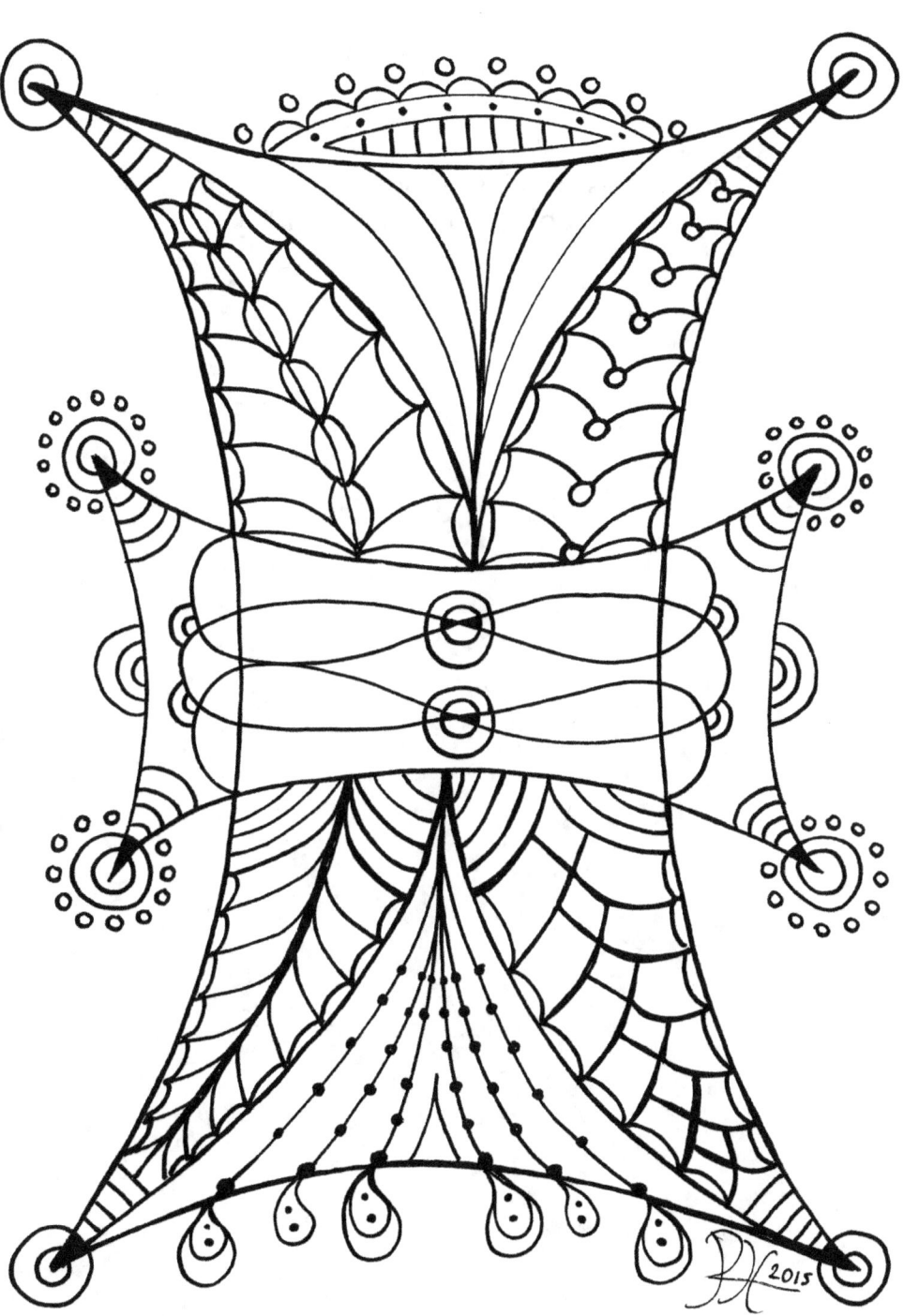

Contributing Artist
DomDomx
France

Facebook : Les-dessins-et-doodles-de-Dom-Domx
Facebook Group : Color.Addict

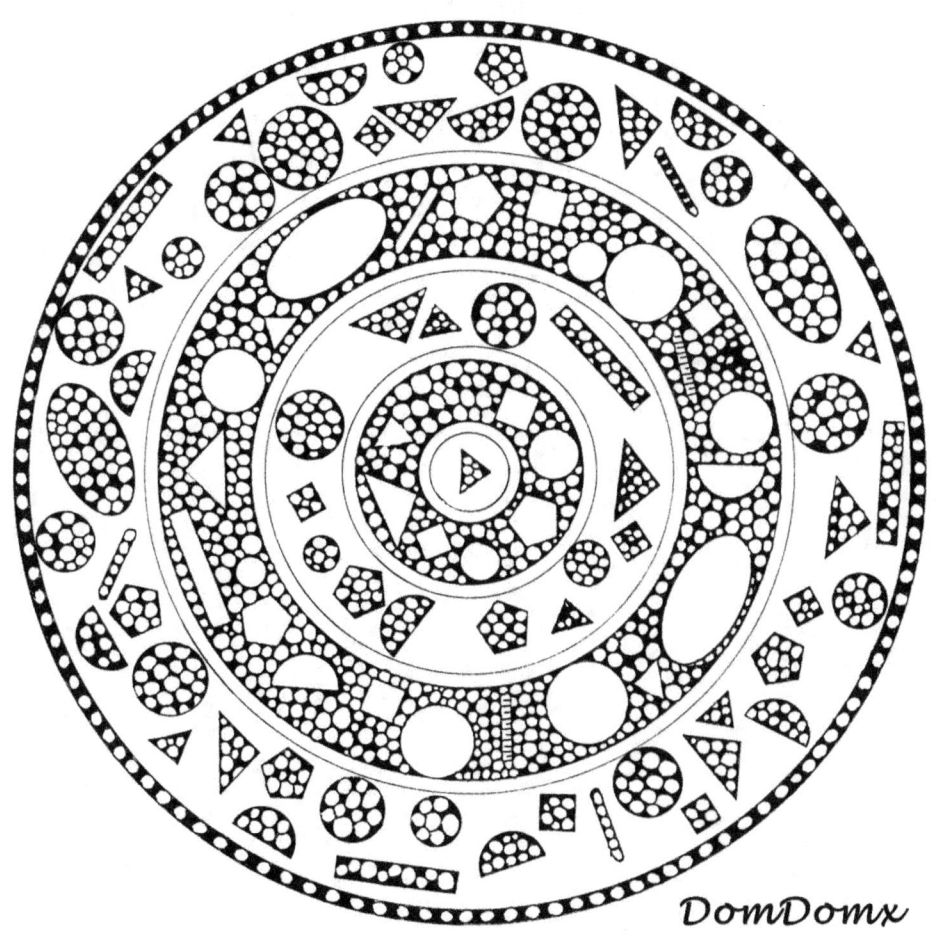

Contributing Artist
Dianne Comeau
Canada

Blog : https://diannecomeau.wordpress.com/

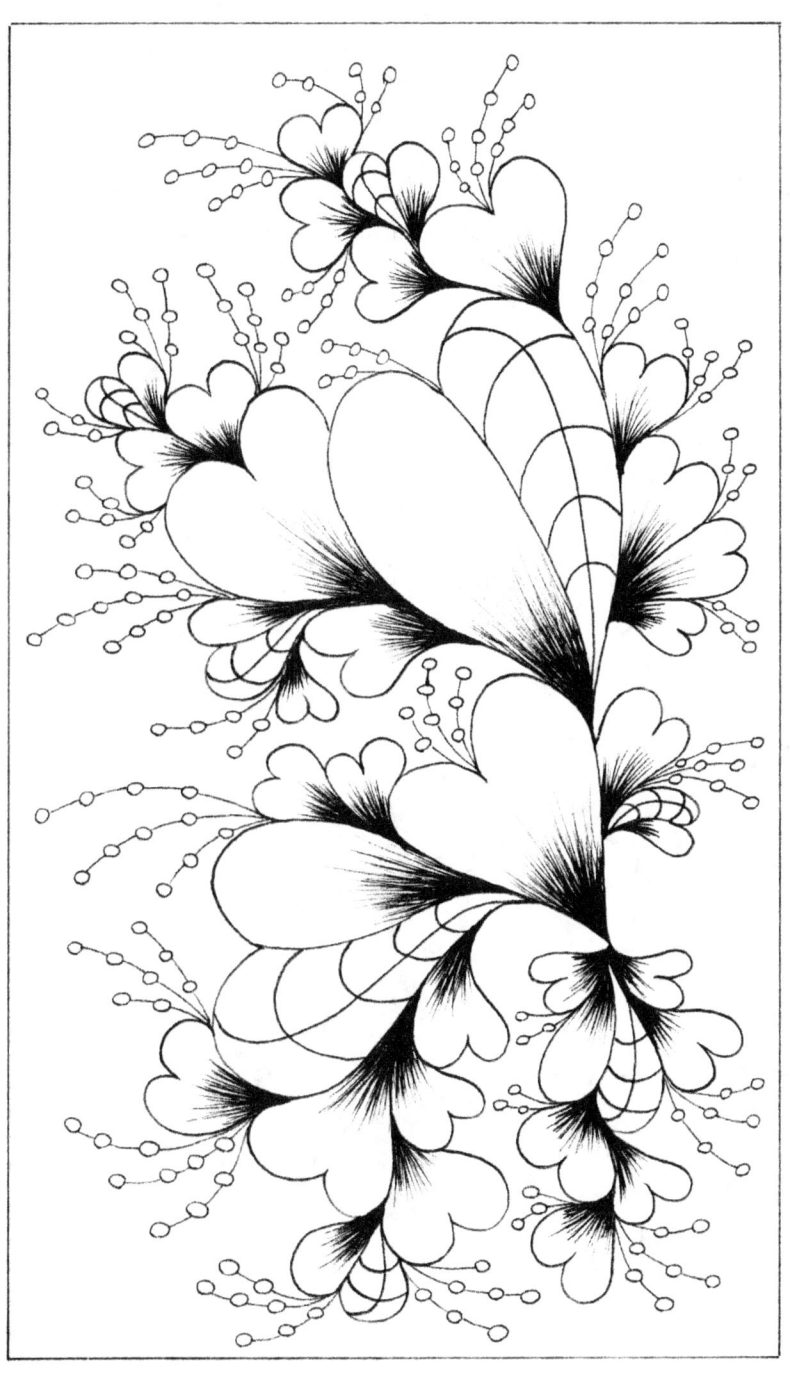

Contributing Artist
Diana Holmes
USA

Facebook : WhimsicalCheers

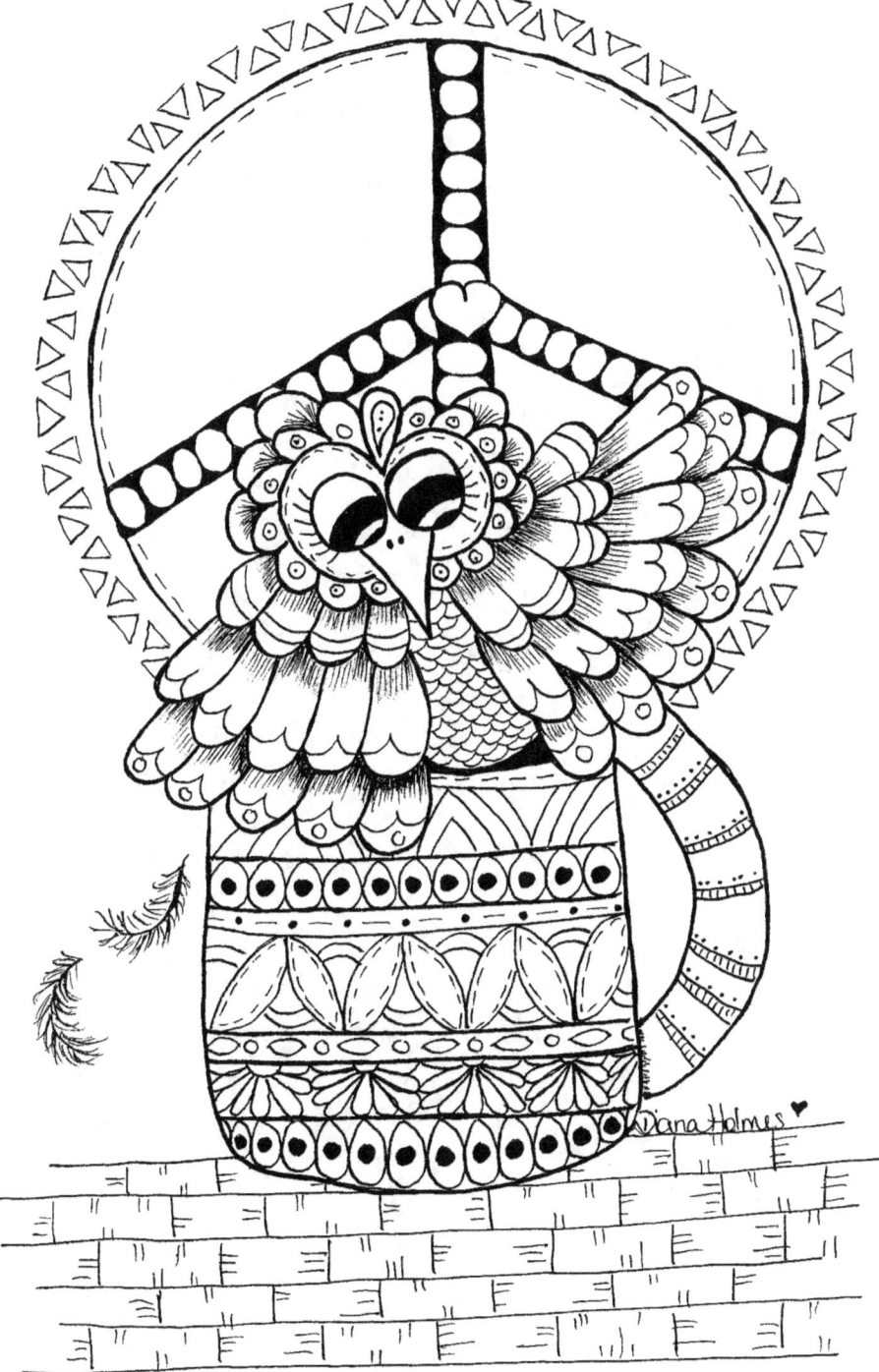

Contributing Artist
Audrey Sagh
Saskatoon, Saskatchewan Canada

Facebook : AMS-Artwork

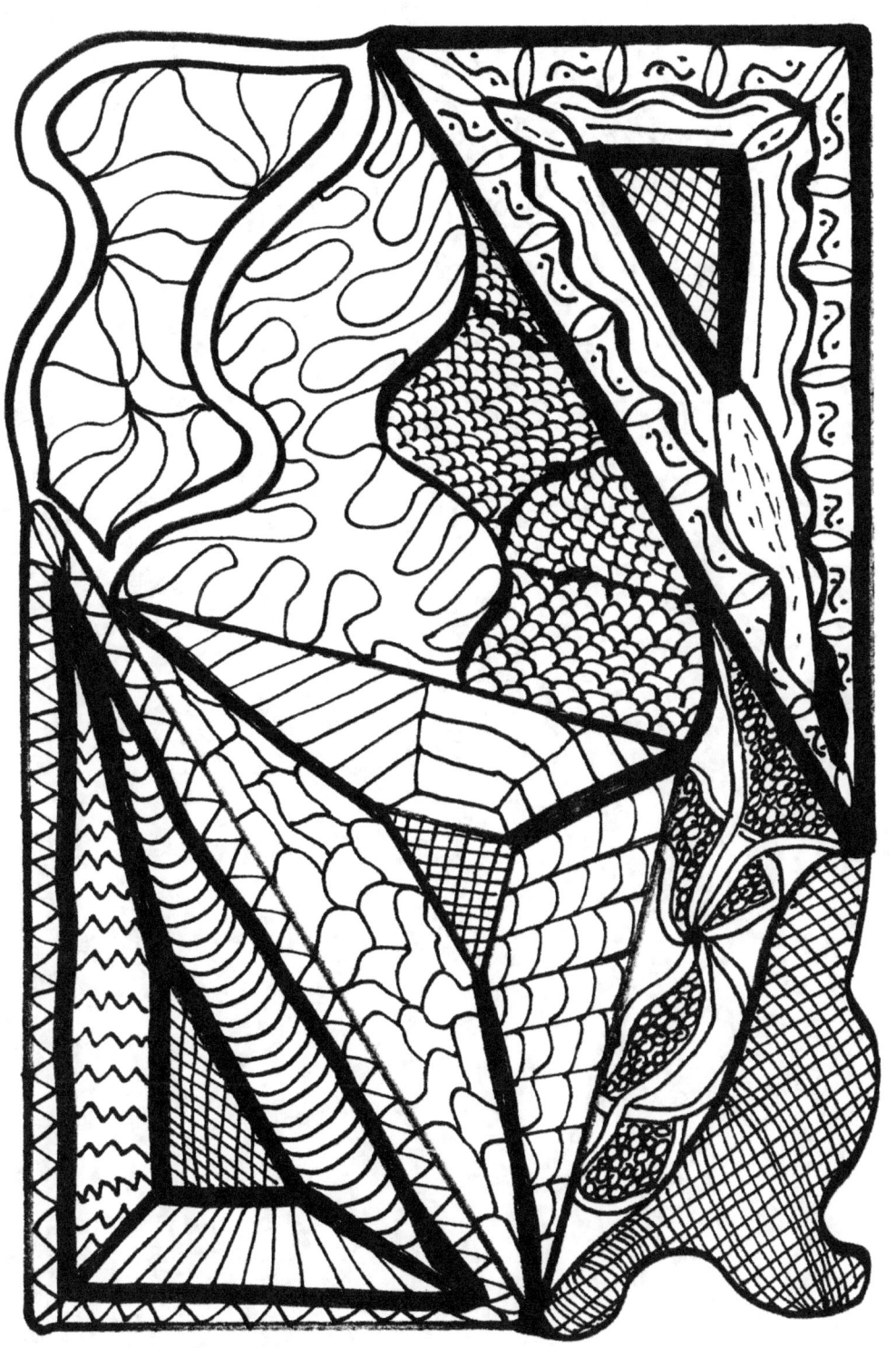

Contributing Artist
Audrey Sagh
Saskatoon, Saskatchewan Canada

Facebook : AMS-Artwork

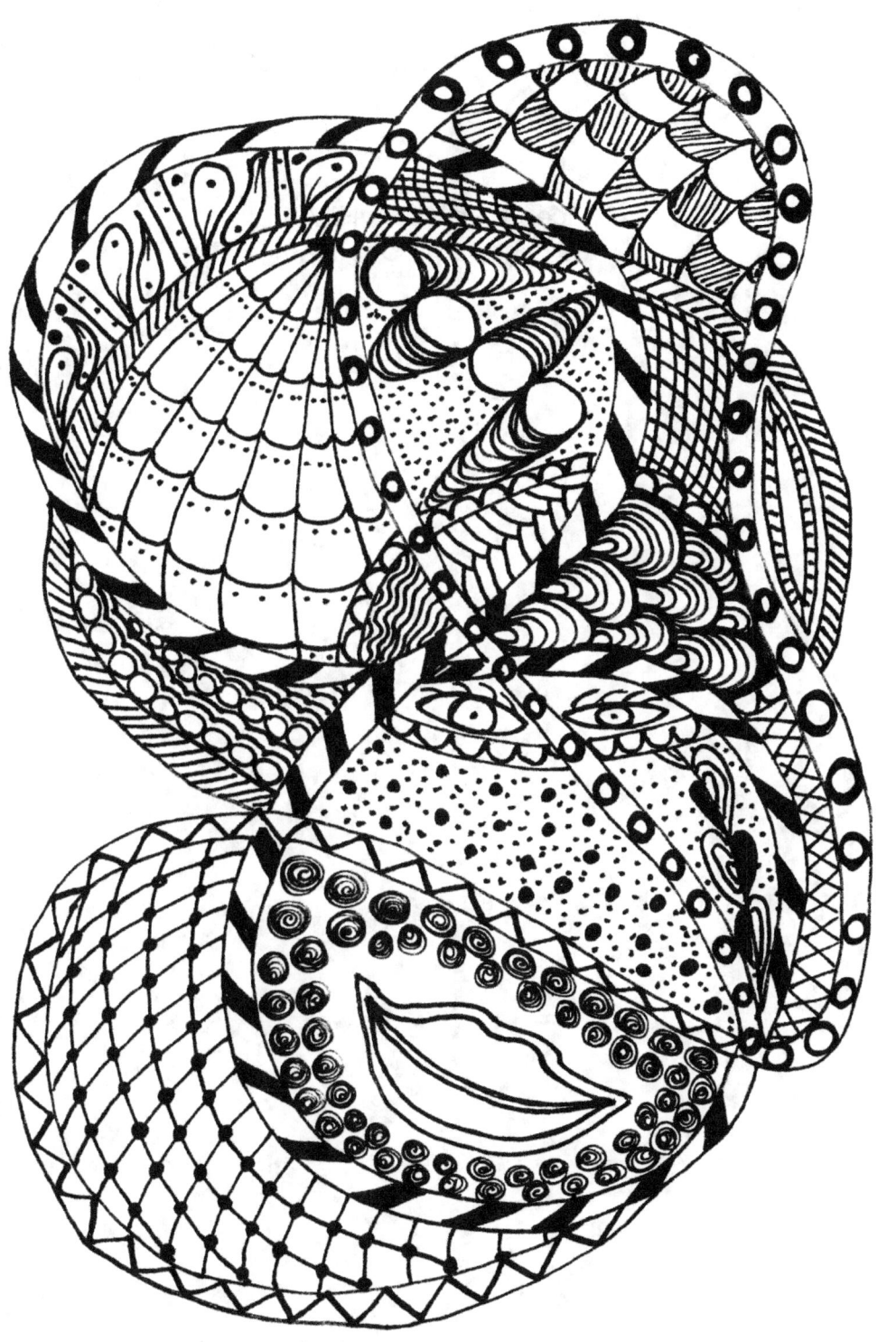

Contributing Artist
Nicole Whelan (Willow Hill Art)
WI, USA

Facebook : WillowHillArt
Etsy shop : WillowHillArt

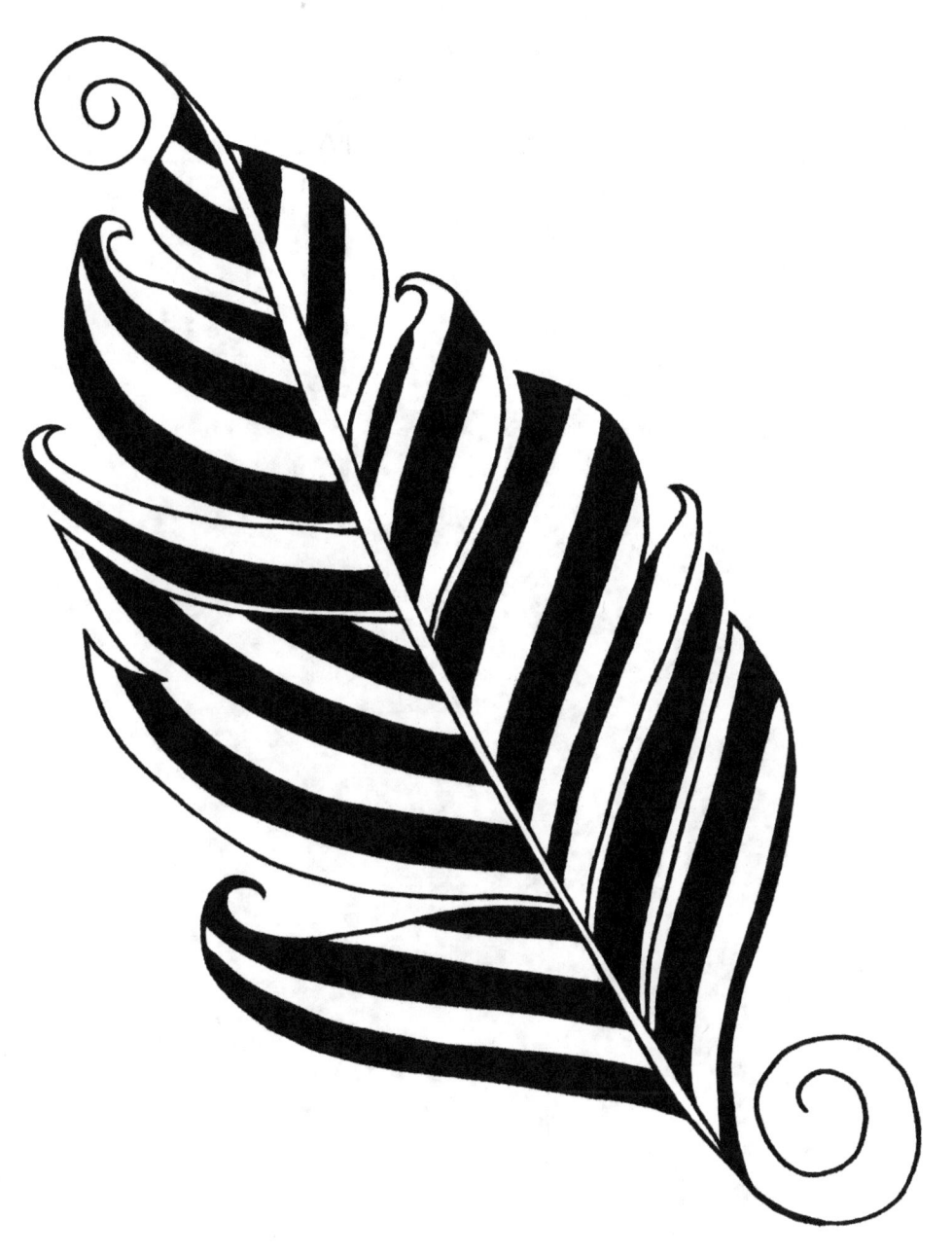

Contributing Artist
Nicole Whelan (Willow Hill Art)
WI, USA

Facebook : WillowHillArt
Etsy shop : WillowHillArt

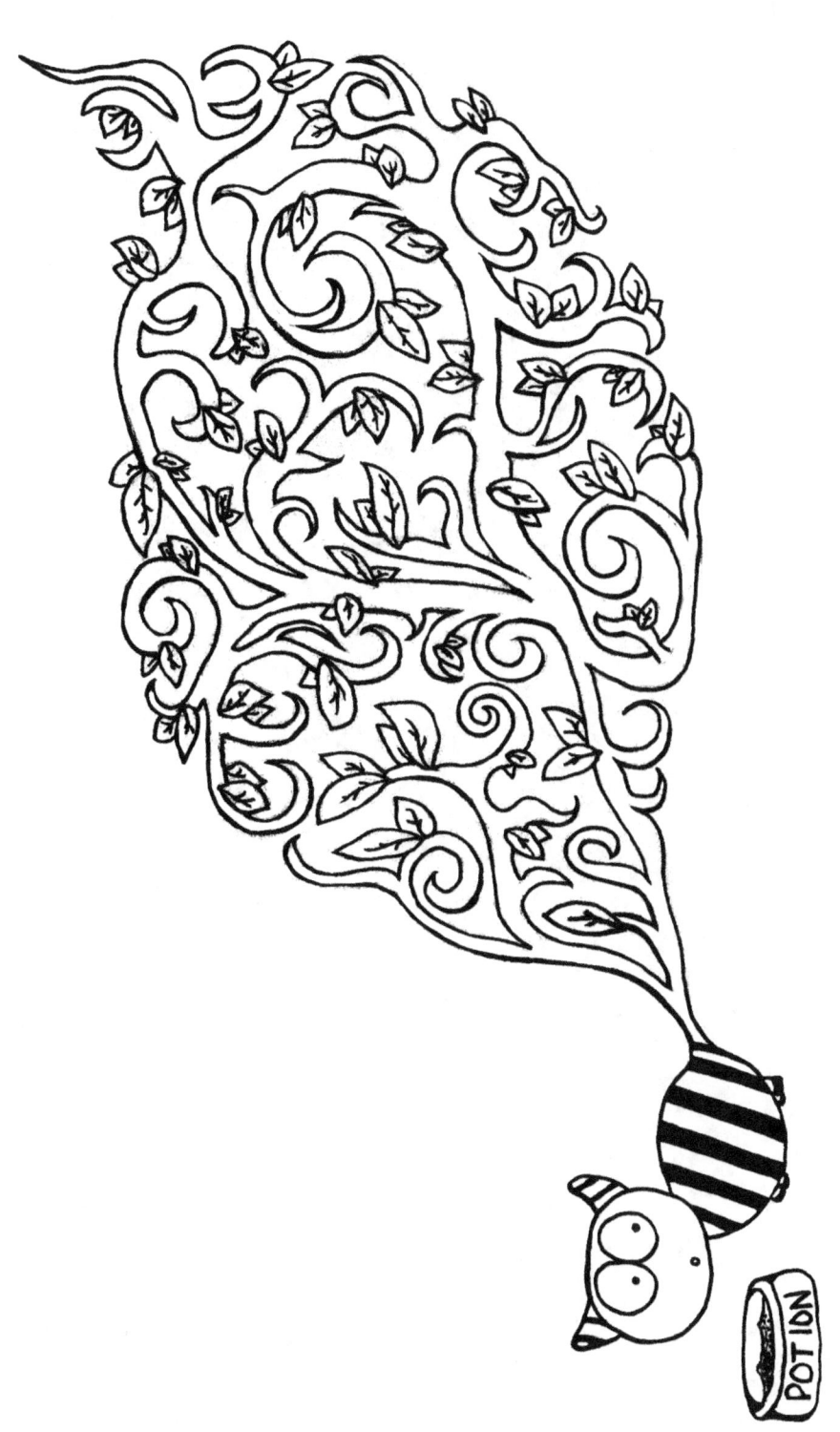

Contributing Artist
Nicole Whelan (Willow Hill Art)
WI, USA

Facebook : WillowHillArt
Etsy shop : WillowHillArt

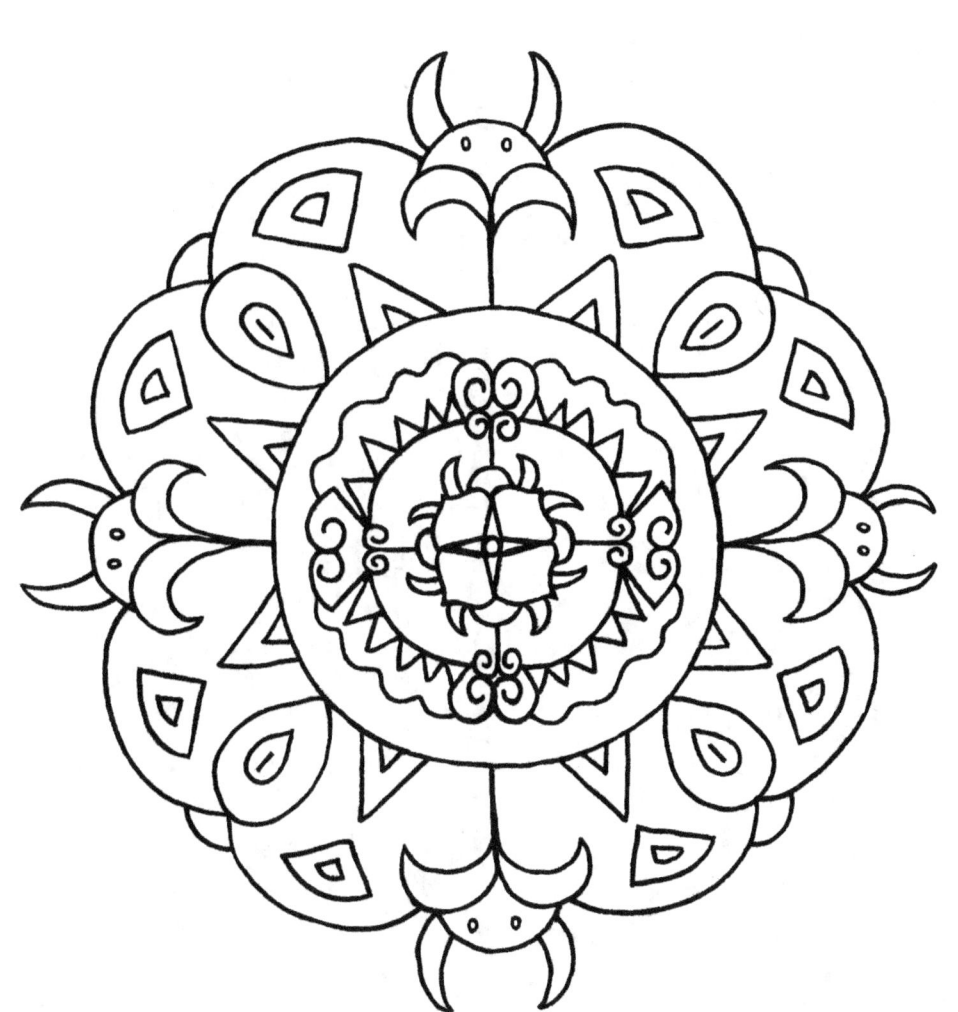

Contributing Artist
Nicole Whelan (Willow Hill Art)
WI, USA

Facebook : WillowHillArt
Etsy shop : WillowHillArt

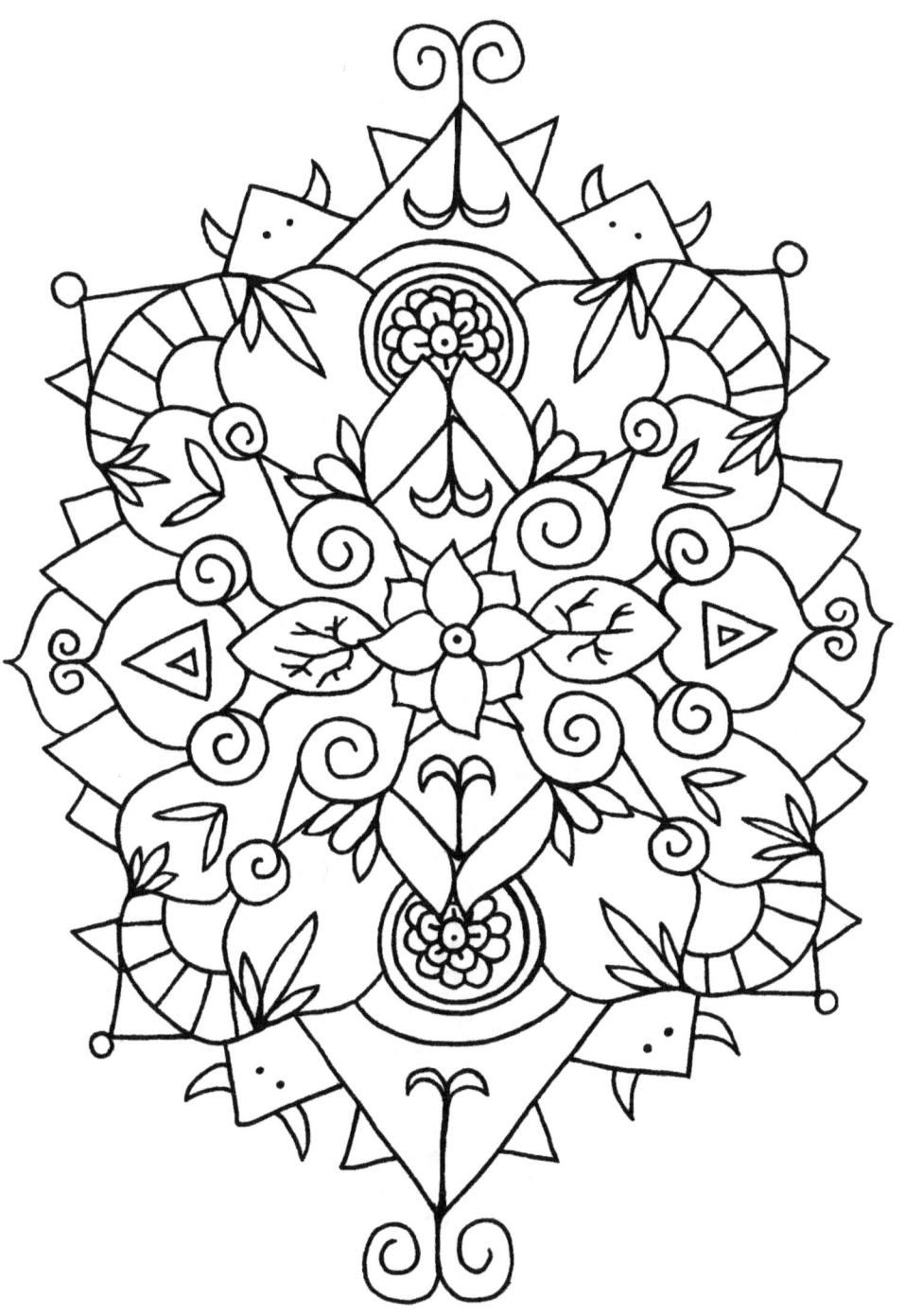

Contributing Artist
Ondine Summers
U.K.

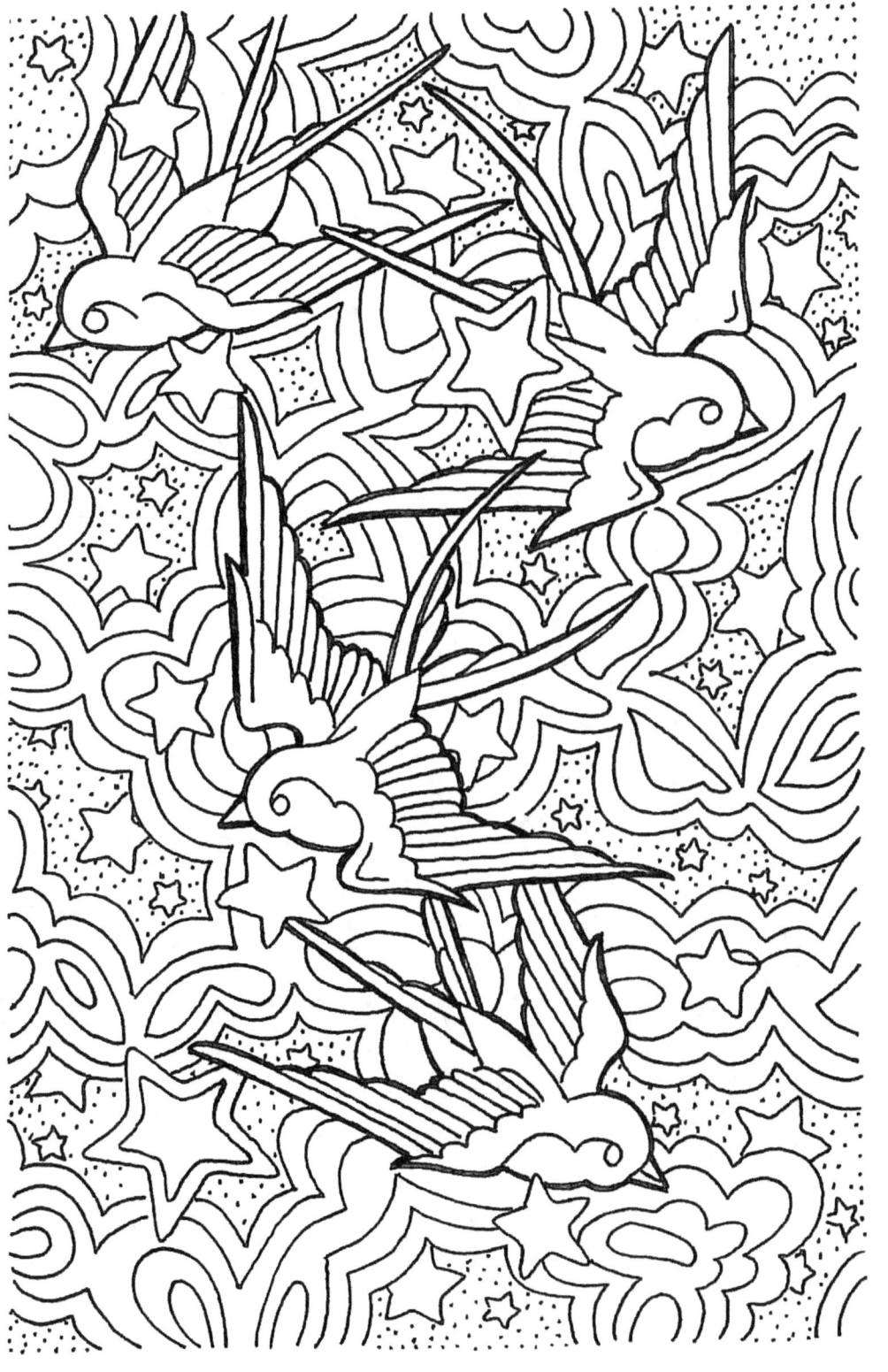

Contributing Artist
Ondine Summers
U.K.

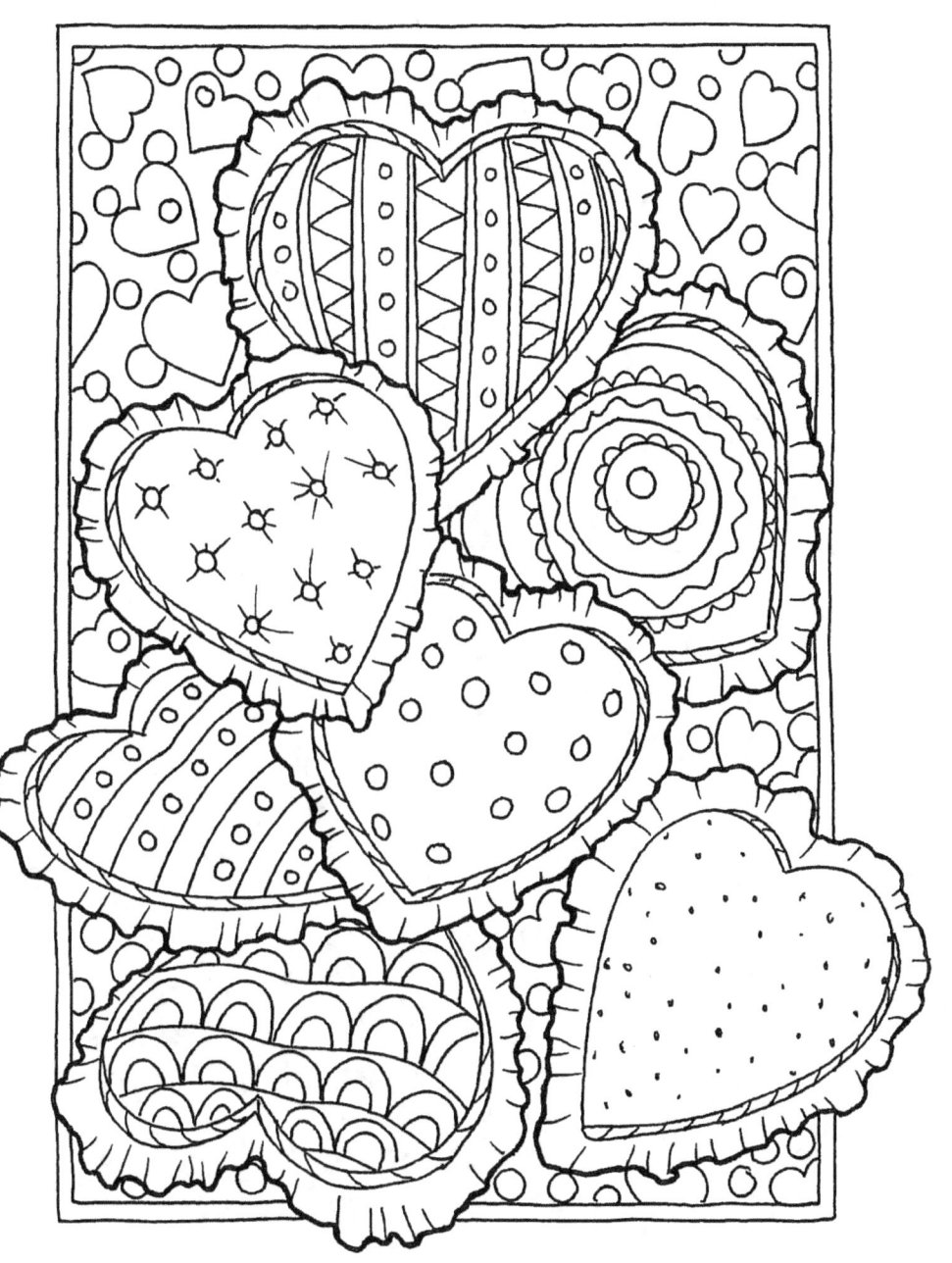

Contributing Artist
Ondine Summers
U.K.

Published by
"GDG"
Global Doodle Gems

Drawn & colored

by

Rover Hsiao

Background Art

Drawn & colored

by

Johanna Ans

Looking forward to presenting the next Mini Collection with 50 more designs !

www.ingramcontent.com/pod-product-compliance
Lightning Source LLC
Chambersburg PA
CBHW050116230526
45470CB00004B/1849